ISBN 0-8373-3507-8

C-3507　CAREER EXAMINATION SERIES

This is your
PASSBOOK® for...

Intergovernmental Analyst

Test Preparation Study Guide

Questions & Answers

NLC

NATIONAL LEARNING CORPORATION

PASSBOOK®

NOTICE

PASSBOOK SERIES®

THE *PASSBOOK SERIES®* has been created to prepare applicants and candidates for the ultimate academic battlefield – the examination room.

At some time in our lives, each and every one of us may be required to take an examination – for validation, matriculation, admission, qualification, registration, certification, or licensure.

Based on the assumption that every applicant or candidate has met the basic formal educational standards, has taken the required number of courses, and read the necessary texts, the *PASSBOOK SERIES®* furnishes the one special preparation which may assure passing with confidence, instead of failing with insecurity. Examination questions – together with answers – are furnished as the basic vehicle for study so that the mysteries of the examination and its compounding difficulties may be eliminated or diminished by a sure method.

This book is meant to help you pass your examination provided that you qualify and are serious in your objective.

The entire field is reviewed through the huge store of content information which is succinctly presented through a provocative and challenging approach – the question-and-answer method.

A climate of success is established by furnishing the correct answers at the end of each test.

You soon learn to recognize types of questions, forms of questions, and patterns of questioning. You may even begin to anticipate expected outcomes.

You perceive that many questions are repeated or adapted so that you can gain acute insights, which may enable you to score many sure points.

You learn how to confront new questions, or types of questions, and to attack them confidently and work out the correct answers.

You note objectives and emphases, and recognize pitfalls and dangers, so that you may make positive educational adjustments.

Moreover, you are kept fully informed in relation to new concepts, methods, practices, and directions in the field.

You discover that you are actually taking the examination all the time: you are preparing for the examination by "taking" an examination, not by reading extraneous and/or supererogatory textbooks.

In short, this PASSBOOK®, used directedly, should be an important factor in helping you to pass your test.

INTERGOVERNMENTAL ANALYST

DUTIES
An employee in this class is involved in performing a variety of entry-level tasks related to organizing and carrying out the county's federal, state and local legislative agendas. Primary responsibility is for providing basic research support for higher-level staff members. The incumbent helps to analyze and monitor legislation at county, state and federal levels, and assists in working with county departments, local governments and special districts to ascertain legislative concerns. Specific assignments are received from supervisors, and work is performed under direct supervision. Does related work as required.

SCOPE OF THE EXAMINATION
The <u>written test</u> will cover knowledge, skills and abilities in such areas as:

1. Arithmetic reasoning;
2. Evaluating conclusions in light of known facts;
3. Preparing written material;
4. Understanding and interpreting tabular material; and
5. Understanding and interpreting written material.

HOW TO TAKE A TEST

I. YOU MUST PASS AN EXAMINATION

A. *WHAT EVERY CANDIDATE SHOULD KNOW*

Examination applicants often ask us for help in preparing for the written test. What can I study in advance? What kinds of questions will be asked? How will the test be given? How will the papers be graded?

As an applicant for a civil service examination, you may be wondering about some of these things. Our purpose here is to suggest effective methods of advance study and to describe civil service examinations.

Your chances for success on this examination can be increased if you know how to prepare. Those "pre-examination jitters" can be reduced if you know what to expect. You can even experience an adventure in good citizenship if you know why civil service exams are given.

B. *WHY ARE CIVIL SERVICE EXAMINATIONS GIVEN?*

Civil service examinations are important to you in two ways. As a citizen, you want public jobs filled by employees who know how to do their work. As a job seeker, you want a fair chance to compete for that job on an equal footing with other candidates. The best-known means of accomplishing this two-fold goal is the competitive examination.

Exams are widely publicized throughout the nation. They may be administered for jobs in federal, state, city, municipal, town or village governments or agencies.

Any citizen may apply, with some limitations, such as the age or residence of applicants. Your experience and education may be reviewed to see whether you meet the requirements for the particular examination. When these requirements exist, they are reasonable and applied consistently to all applicants. Thus, a competitive examination may cause you some uneasiness now, but it is your privilege and safeguard.

C. *HOW ARE CIVIL SERVICE EXAMS DEVELOPED?*

Examinations are carefully written by trained technicians who are specialists in the field known as "psychological measurement," in consultation with recognized authorities in the field of work that the test will cover. These experts recommend the subject matter areas or skills to be tested; only those knowledges or skills important to your success on the job are included. The most reliable books and source materials available are used as references. Together, the experts and technicians judge the difficulty level of the questions.

Test technicians know how to phrase questions so that the problem is clearly stated. Their ethics do not permit "trick" or "catch" questions. Questions may have been tried out on sample groups, or subjected to statistical analysis, to determine their usefulness.

Written tests are often used in combination with performance tests, ratings of training and experience, and oral interviews. All of these measures combine to form the best-known means of finding the right person for the right job.

II. HOW TO PASS THE WRITTEN TEST

A. NATURE OF THE EXAMINATION

To prepare intelligently for civil service examinations, you should know how they differ from school examinations you have taken. In school you were assigned certain definite pages to read or subjects to cover. The examination questions were quite detailed and usually emphasized memory. Civil service exams, on the other hand, try to discover your present ability to perform the duties of a position, plus your potentiality to learn these duties. In other words, a civil service exam attempts to predict how successful you will be. Questions cover such a broad area that they cannot be as minute and detailed as school exam questions.

In the public service similar kinds of work, or positions, are grouped together in one "class." This process is known as *position-classification*. All the positions in a class are paid according to the salary range for that class. One class title covers all of these positions, and they are all tested by the same examination.

B. FOUR BASIC STEPS

1) Study the announcement

How, then, can you know what subjects to study? Our best answer is: "Learn as much as possible about the class of positions for which you've applied." The exam will test the knowledge, skills and abilities needed to do the work.

Your most valuable source of information about the position you want is the official exam announcement. This announcement lists the training and experience qualifications. Check these standards and apply only if you come reasonably close to meeting them.

The brief description of the position in the examination announcement offers some clues to the subjects which will be tested. Think about the job itself. Review the duties in your mind. Can you perform them, or are there some in which you are rusty? Fill in the blank spots in your preparation.

Many jurisdictions preview the written test in the exam announcement by including a section called "Knowledge and Abilities Required," "Scope of the Examination," or some similar heading. Here you will find out specifically what fields will be tested.

2) Review your own background

Once you learn in general what the position is all about, and what you need to know to do the work, ask yourself which subjects you already know fairly well and which need improvement. You may wonder whether to concentrate on improving your strong areas or on building some background in your fields of weakness. When the announcement has specified "some knowledge" or "considerable knowledge," or has used adjectives like "beginning principles of..." or "advanced ... methods," you can get a clue as to the number and difficulty of questions to be asked in any given field. More questions, and hence broader coverage, would be included for those subjects which are more important in the work. Now weigh your strengths and weaknesses against the job requirements and prepare accordingly.

3) Determine the level of the position

Another way to tell how intensively you should prepare is to understand the level of the job for which you are applying. Is it the entering level? In other words, is this the position in which beginners in a field of work are hired? Or is it an intermediate or advanced level? Sometimes this is indicated by such words as "Junior" or "Senior" in the class title. Other jurisdictions use Roman numerals to designate the level – Clerk I, Clerk II, for example. The word "Supervisor" sometimes appears in the title. If the level is not indicated by the title, check the description of duties. Will you be working under very close supervision, or will you have responsibility for independent decisions in this work?

4) Choose appropriate study materials

Now that you know the subjects to be examined and the relative amount of each subject to be covered, you can choose suitable study materials. For beginning level jobs, or even advanced ones, if you have a pronounced weakness in some aspect of your training, read a modern, standard textbook in that field. Be sure it is up to date and has general coverage. Such books are normally available at your library, and the librarian will be glad to help you locate one. For entry-level positions, questions of appropriate difficulty are chosen – neither highly advanced questions, nor those too simple. Such questions require careful thought but not advanced training.

If the position for which you are applying is technical or advanced, you will read more advanced, specialized material. If you are already familiar with the basic principles of your field, elementary textbooks would waste your time. Concentrate on advanced textbooks and technical periodicals. Think through the concepts and review difficult problems in your field.

These are all general sources. You can get more ideas on your own initiative, following these leads. For example, training manuals and publications of the government agency which employs workers in your field can be useful, particularly for technical and professional positions. A letter or visit to the government department involved may result in more specific study suggestions, and certainly will provide you with a more definite idea of the exact nature of the position you are seeking.

III. KINDS OF TESTS

Tests are used for purposes other than measuring knowledge and ability to perform specified duties. For some positions, it is equally important to test ability to make adjustments to new situations or to profit from training. In others, basic mental abilities not dependent on information are essential. Questions which test these things may not appear as pertinent to the duties of the position as those which test for knowledge and information. Yet they are often highly important parts of a fair examination. For very general questions, it is almost impossible to help you direct your study efforts. What we can do is to point out some of the more common of these general abilities needed in public service positions and describe some typical questions.

1) General information

Broad, general information has been found useful for predicting job success in some kinds of work. This is tested in a variety of ways, from vocabulary lists to questions about current events. Basic background in some field of work, such as sociology or economics, may be sampled in a group of questions. Often these are principles which have become familiar to most persons through exposure rather than through formal training. It is difficult to advise you how to study for these questions; being alert to the world around you is our best suggestion.

2) Verbal ability

An example of an ability needed in many positions is verbal or language ability. Verbal ability is, in brief, the ability to use and understand words. Vocabulary and grammar tests are typical measures of this ability. Reading comprehension or paragraph interpretation questions are common in many kinds of civil service tests. You are given a paragraph of written material and asked to find its central meaning.

3) Numerical ability

Number skills can be tested by the familiar arithmetic problem, by checking paired lists of numbers to see which are alike and which are different, or by interpreting charts and graphs. In the latter test, a graph may be printed in the test booklet which you are asked to use as the basis for answering questions.

4) Observation

A popular test for law-enforcement positions is the observation test. A picture is shown to you for several minutes, then taken away. Questions about the picture test your ability to observe both details and larger elements.

5) Following directions

In many positions in the public service, the employee must be able to carry out written instructions dependably and accurately. You may be given a chart with several columns, each column listing a variety of information. The questions require you to carry out directions involving the information given in the chart.

6) Skills and aptitudes

Performance tests effectively measure some manual skills and aptitudes. When the skill is one in which you are trained, such as typing or shorthand, you can practice. These tests are often very much like those given in business school or high school courses. For many of the other skills and aptitudes, however, no short-time preparation can be made. Skills and abilities natural to you or that you have developed throughout your lifetime are being tested.

Many of the general questions just described provide all the data needed to answer the questions and ask you to use your reasoning ability to find the answers. Your best preparation for these tests, as well as for tests of facts and ideas, is to be at your physical and mental best. You, no doubt, have your own methods of getting into an exam-taking mood and keeping "in shape." The next section lists some ideas on this subject.

IV. KINDS OF QUESTIONS

Only rarely is the "essay" question, which you answer in narrative form, used in civil service tests. Civil service tests are usually of the short-answer type. Full instructions for answering these questions will be given to you at the examination. But in case this is your first experience with short-answer questions and separate answer sheets, here is what you need to know:

1) Multiple-choice Questions

Most popular of the short-answer questions is the "multiple choice" or "best answer" question. It can be used, for example, to test for factual knowledge, ability to solve problems or judgment in meeting situations found at work.

A multiple-choice question is normally one of three types—

- It can begin with an incomplete statement followed by several possible endings. You are to find the one ending which *best* completes the statement, although some of the others may not be entirely wrong.
- It can also be a complete statement in the form of a question which is answered by choosing one of the statements listed.
- It can be in the form of a problem – again you select the best answer.

Here is an example of a multiple-choice question with a discussion which should give you some clues as to the method for choosing the right answer:

When an employee has a complaint about his assignment, the action which will *best* help him overcome his difficulty is to
- A. discuss his difficulty with his coworkers
- B. take the problem to the head of the organization
- C. take the problem to the person who gave him the assignment
- D. say nothing to anyone about his complaint

In answering this question, you should study each of the choices to find which is best. Consider choice "A" – Certainly an employee may discuss his complaint with fellow employees, but no change or improvement can result, and the complaint remains unresolved. Choice "B" is a poor choice since the head of the organization probably does not know what assignment you have been given, and taking your problem to him is known as "going over the head" of the supervisor. The supervisor, or person who made the assignment, is the person who can clarify it or correct any injustice. Choice "C" is, therefore, correct. To say nothing, as in choice "D," is unwise. Supervisors have and interest in knowing the problems employees are facing, and the employee is seeking a solution to his problem.

2) True/False Questions

The "true/false" or "right/wrong" form of question is sometimes used. Here a complete statement is given. Your job is to decide whether the statement is right or wrong.

SAMPLE: A person-to-person long-distance telephone call costs less than a station-to-station call to the same city.

This statement is wrong, or false, since person-to-person calls are more expensive.

This is not a complete list of all possible question forms, although most of the others are variations of these common types. You will always get complete directions for answering questions. Be sure you understand *how* to mark your answers – ask questions until you do.

V. RECORDING YOUR ANSWERS

For an examination with very few applicants, you may be told to record your answers in the test booklet itself. Separate answer sheets are much more common. If this separate answer sheet is to be scored by machine – and this is often the case – it is highly important that you mark your answers correctly in order to get credit.

An electric scoring machine is often used in civil service offices because of the speed with which papers can be scored. Machine-scored answer sheets must be marked with a pencil, which will be given to you. This pencil has a high graphite content which responds to the electric scoring machine. As a matter of fact, stray dots may register as answers, so do not let your pencil rest on the answer sheet while you are pondering the correct answer. Also, if your pencil lead breaks or is otherwise defective, ask for another.

Since the answer sheet will be dropped in a slot in the scoring machine, be careful not to bend the corners or get the paper crumpled.

The answer sheet normally has five vertical columns of numbers, with 30 numbers to a column. These numbers correspond to the question numbers in your test booklet. After each number, going across the page are four or five pairs of dotted lines. These short dotted lines have small letters or numbers above them. The first two pairs may also have a "T" or "F" above the letters. This indicates that the first two pairs only are to be used if the questions are of the true-false type. If the questions are multiple choice, disregard the "T" and "F" and pay attention only to the small letters or numbers.

Answer your questions in the manner of the sample that follows:

32. The largest city in the United States is
    A. Washington, D.C.
    B. New York City
    C. Chicago
    D. Detroit
    E. San Francisco

1) Choose the answer you think is best. (New York City is the largest, so "B" is correct.)
2) Find the row of dotted lines numbered the same as the question you are answering. (Find row number 32)
3) Find the pair of dotted lines corresponding to the answer. (Find the pair of lines under the mark "B.")
4) Make a solid black mark between the dotted lines.

VI. BEFORE THE TEST

Common sense will help you find procedures to follow to get ready for an examination. Too many of us, however, overlook these sensible measures. Indeed, nervousness and fatigue have been found to be the most serious reasons why applicants fail to do their best on civil service tests. Here is a list of reminders:

- Begin your preparation early – Don't wait until the last minute to go scurrying around for books and materials or to find out what the position is all about.
- Prepare continuously – An hour a night for a week is better than an all-night cram session. This has been definitely established. What is more, a night a

week for a month will return better dividends than crowding your study into a shorter period of time.

- Locate the place of the exam – You have been sent a notice telling you when and where to report for the examination. If the location is in a different town or otherwise unfamiliar to you, it would be well to inquire the best route and learn something about the building.
- Relax the night before the test – Allow your mind to rest. Do not study at all that night. Plan some mild recreation or diversion; then go to bed early and get a good night's sleep.
- Get up early enough to make a leisurely trip to the place for the test – This way unforeseen events, traffic snarls, unfamiliar buildings, etc. will not upset you.
- Dress comfortably – A written test is not a fashion show. You will be known by number and not by name, so wear something comfortable.
- Leave excess paraphernalia at home – Shopping bags and odd bundles will get in your way. You need bring only the items mentioned in the official notice you received; usually everything you need is provided. Do not bring reference books to the exam. They will only confuse those last minutes and be taken away from you when in the test room.
- Arrive somewhat ahead of time – If because of transportation schedules you must get there very early, bring a newspaper or magazine to take your mind off yourself while waiting.
- Locate the examination room – When you have found the proper room, you will be directed to the seat or part of the room where you will sit. Sometimes you are given a sheet of instructions to read while you are waiting. Do not fill out any forms until you are told to do so; just read them and be prepared.
- Relax and prepare to listen to the instructions
- If you have any physical problem that may keep you from doing your best, be sure to tell the test administrator. If you are sick or in poor health, you really cannot do your best on the exam. You can come back and take the test some other time.

VII. AT THE TEST

The day of the test is here and you have the test booklet in your hand. The temptation to get going is very strong. Caution! There is more to success than knowing the right answers. You must know how to identify your papers and understand variations in the type of short-answer question used in this particular examination. Follow these suggestions for maximum results from your efforts:

1) Cooperate with the monitor

The test administrator has a duty to create a situation in which you can be as much at ease as possible. He will give instructions, tell you when to begin, check to see that you are marking your answer sheet correctly, and so on. He is not there to guard you, although he will see that your competitors do not take unfair advantage. He wants to help you do your best.

2) Listen to all instructions

Don't jump the gun! Wait until you understand all directions. In most civil service tests you get more time than you need to answer the questions. So don't be in a hurry.

Read each word of instructions until you clearly understand the meaning. Study the examples, listen to all announcements and follow directions. Ask questions if you do not understand what to do.

3) Identify your papers

Civil service exams are usually identified by number only. You will be assigned a number; you must not put your name on your test papers. Be sure to copy your number correctly. Since more than one exam may be given, copy your exact examination title.

4) Plan your time

Unless you are told that a test is a "speed" or "rate of work" test, speed itself is usually not important. Time enough to answer all the questions will be provided, but this does not mean that you have all day. An overall time limit has been set. Divide the total time (in minutes) by the number of questions to determine the approximate time you have for each question.

5) Do not linger over difficult questions

If you come across a difficult question, mark it with a paper clip (useful to have along) and come back to it when you have been through the booklet. One caution if you do this – be sure to skip a number on your answer sheet as well. Check often to be sure that you have not lost your place and that you are marking in the row numbered the same as the question you are answering.

6) Read the questions

Be sure you know what the question asks! Many capable people are unsuccessful because they failed to *read* the questions correctly.

7) Answer all questions

Unless you have been instructed that a penalty will be deducted for incorrect answers, it is better to guess than to omit a question.

8) Speed tests

It is often better NOT to guess on speed tests. It has been found that on timed tests people are tempted to spend the last few seconds before time is called in marking answers at random – without even reading them – in the hope of picking up a few extra points. To discourage this practice, the instructions may warn you that your score will be "corrected" for guessing. That is, a penalty will be applied. The incorrect answers will be deducted from the correct ones, or some other penalty formula will be used.

9) Review your answers

If you finish before time is called, go back to the questions you guessed or omitted to give them further thought. Review other answers if you have time.

10) Return your test materials

If you are ready to leave before others have finished or time is called, take ALL your materials to the monitor and leave quietly. Never take any test material with you. The monitor can discover whose papers are not complete, and taking a test booklet may be grounds for disqualification.

VIII. EXAMINATION TECHNIQUES

1) Read the general instructions carefully. These are usually printed on the first page of the exam booklet. As a rule, these instructions refer to the timing of the examination; the fact that you should not start work until the signal and must stop work at a signal, etc. If there are any *special* instructions, such as a choice of questions to be answered, make sure that you note this instruction carefully.

2) When you are ready to start work on the examination, that is as soon as the signal has been given, read the instructions to each question booklet, underline any key words or phrases, such as *least, best, outline, describe* and the like. In this way you will tend to answer as requested rather than discover on reviewing your paper that you *listed without describing*, that you selected the *worst* choice rather than the *best* choice, etc.

3) If the examination is of the objective or multiple-choice type – that is, each question will also give a series of possible answers: A, B, C or D, and you are called upon to select the best answer and write the letter next to that answer on your answer paper – it is advisable to start answering each question in turn. There may be anywhere from 50 to 100 such questions in the three or four hours allotted and you can see how much time would be taken if you read through all the questions before beginning to answer any. Furthermore, if you come across a question or group of questions which you know would be difficult to answer, it would undoubtedly affect your handling of all the other questions.

4) If the examination is of the essay type and contains but a few questions, it is a moot point as to whether you should read all the questions before starting to answer any one. Of course, if you are given a choice – say five out of seven and the like – then it is essential to read all the questions so you can eliminate the two that are most difficult. If, however, you are asked to answer all the questions, there may be danger in trying to answer the easiest one first because you may find that you will spend too much time on it. The best technique is to answer the first question, then proceed to the second, etc.

5) Time your answers. Before the exam begins, write down the time it started, then add the time allowed for the examination and write down the time it must be completed, then divide the time available somewhat as follows:
   - If 3-1/2 hours are allowed, that would be 210 minutes. If you have 80 objective-type questions, that would be an average of 2-1/2 minutes per question. Allow yourself no more than 2 minutes per question, or a total of 160 minutes, which will permit about 50 minutes to review.
   - If for the time allotment of 210 minutes there are 7 essay questions to answer, that would average about 30 minutes a question. Give yourself only 25 minutes per question so that you have about 35 minutes to review.

6) The most important instruction is to *read each question* and make sure you know what is wanted. The second most important instruction is to *time yourself properly* so that you answer every question. The third most

important instruction is to *answer every question.* Guess if you have to but include something for each question. Remember that you will receive no credit for a blank and will probably receive some credit if you write something in answer to an essay question. If you guess a letter – say "B" for a multiple-choice question – you may have guessed right. If you leave a blank as an answer to a multiple-choice question, the examiners may respect your feelings but it will not add a point to your score. Some exams may penalize you for wrong answers, so in such cases *only,* you may not want to guess unless you have some basis for your answer.

7) Suggestions
   a. Objective-type questions
      1. Examine the question booklet for proper sequence of pages and questions
      2. Read all instructions carefully
      3. Skip any question which seems too difficult; return to it after all other questions have been answered
      4. Apportion your time properly; do not spend too much time on any single question or group of questions
      5. Note and underline key words – *all, most, fewest, least, best, worst, same, opposite,* etc.
      6. Pay particular attention to negatives
      7. Note unusual option, e.g., unduly long, short, complex, different or similar in content to the body of the question
      8. Observe the use of "hedging" words – *probably, may, most likely,* etc.
      9. Make sure that your answer is put next to the same number as the question
      10. Do not second-guess unless you have good reason to believe the second answer is definitely more correct
      11. Cross out original answer if you decide another answer is more accurate; do not erase until you are ready to hand your paper in
      12. Answer all questions; guess unless instructed otherwise
      13. Leave time for review

   b. Essay questions
      1. Read each question carefully
      2. Determine exactly what is wanted. Underline key words or phrases.
      3. Decide on outline or paragraph answer
      4. Include many different points and elements unless asked to develop any one or two points or elements
      5. Show impartiality by giving pros and cons unless directed to select one side only
      6. Make and write down any assumptions you find necessary to answer the questions
      7. Watch your English, grammar, punctuation and choice of words
      8. Time your answers; don't crowd material

8) Answering the essay question

Most essay questions can be answered by framing the specific response around several key words or ideas. Here are a few such key words or ideas:

M's: manpower, materials, methods, money, management
P's: purpose, program, policy, plan, procedure, practice, problems, pitfalls, personnel, public relations

   a. Six basic steps in handling problems:
1. Preliminary plan and background development
2. Collect information, data and facts
3. Analyze and interpret information, data and facts
4. Analyze and develop solutions as well as make recommendations
5. Prepare report and sell recommendations
6. Install recommendations and follow up effectiveness

   b. Pitfalls to avoid
1. *Taking things for granted* – A statement of the situation does not necessarily imply that each of the elements is necessarily true; for example, a complaint may be invalid and biased so that all that can be taken for granted is that a complaint has been registered
2. *Considering only one side of a situation* – Wherever possible, indicate several alternatives and then point out the reasons you selected the best one
3. *Failing to indicate follow up* – Whenever your answer indicates action on your part, make certain that you will take proper follow-up action to see how successful your recommendations, procedures or actions turn out to be
4. *Taking too long in answering any single question* – Remember to time your answers properly

IX. AFTER THE TEST

Scoring procedures differ in detail among civil service jurisdictions although the general principles are the same. Whether the papers are hand-scored or graded by machine we have described, they are nearly always graded by number. That is, the person who marks the paper knows only the number – never the name – of the applicant. Not until all the papers have been graded will they be matched with names. If other tests, such as training and experience or oral interview ratings have been given, scores will be combined. Different parts of the examination usually have different weights. For example, the written test might count 60 percent of the final grade, and a rating of training and experience 40 percent. In many jurisdictions, veterans will have a certain number of points added to their grades.

After the final grade has been determined, the names are placed in grade order and an eligible list is established. There are various methods for resolving ties between those who get the same final grade – probably the most common is to place first the name of the person whose application was received first. Job offers are made from the eligible list in the order the names appear on it. You will be notified of your grade and your rank as soon as all these computations have been made. This will be done as rapidly as possible.

People who are found to meet the requirements in the announcement are called "eligibles." Their names are put on a list of eligible candidates. An eligible's chances of getting a job depend on how high he stands on this list and how fast agencies are filling jobs from the list.

When a job is to be filled from a list of eligibles, the agency asks for the names of people on the list of eligibles for that job. When the civil service commission receives this request, it sends to the agency the names of the three people highest on this list. Or, if the job to be filled has specialized requirements, the office sends the agency the names of the top three persons who meet these requirements from the general list.

The appointing officer makes a choice from among the three people whose names were sent to him. If the selected person accepts the appointment, the names of the others are put back on the list to be considered for future openings.

That is the rule in hiring from all kinds of eligible lists, whether they are for typist, carpenter, chemist, or something else. For every vacancy, the appointing officer has his choice of any one of the top three eligibles on the list. This explains why the person whose name is on top of the list sometimes does not get an appointment when some of the persons lower on the list do. If the appointing officer chooses the second or third eligible, the No. 1 eligible does not get a job at once, but stays on the list until he is appointed or the list is terminated.

X. HOW TO PASS THE INTERVIEW TEST

The examination for which you applied requires an oral interview test. You have already taken the written test and you are now being called for the interview test – the final part of the formal examination.

You may think that it is not possible to prepare for an interview test and that there are no procedures to follow during an interview. Our purpose is to point out some things you can do in advance that will help you and some good rules to follow and pitfalls to avoid while you are being interviewed.

What is an interview supposed to test?

The written examination is designed to test the technical knowledge and competence of the candidate; the oral is designed to evaluate intangible qualities, not readily measured otherwise, and to establish a list showing the relative fitness of each candidate – as measured against his competitors – for the position sought. Scoring is not on the basis of "right" and "wrong," but on a sliding scale of values ranging from "not passable" to "outstanding." As a matter of fact, it is possible to achieve a relatively low score without a single "incorrect" answer because of evident weakness in the qualities being measured.

Occasionally, an examination may consist entirely of an oral test – either an individual or a group oral. In such cases, information is sought concerning the technical knowledges and abilities of the candidate, since there has been no written examination for this purpose. More commonly, however, an oral test is used to supplement a written examination.

Who conducts interviews?

The composition of oral boards varies among different jurisdictions. In nearly all, a representative of the personnel department serves as chairman. One of the members of the board may be a representative of the department in which the candidate would work. In some cases, "outside experts" are used, and, frequently, a businessman or some other representative of the general public is asked to serve. Labor and management or other special groups may be represented. The aim is to secure the services of experts in the appropriate field.

However the board is composed, it is a good idea (and not at all improper or unethical) to ascertain in advance of the interview who the members are and what groups they represent. When you are introduced to them, you will have some idea of their backgrounds and interests, and at least you will not stutter and stammer over their names.

What should be done before the interview?

While knowledge about the board members is useful and takes some of the surprise element out of the interview, there is other preparation which is more substantive. It *is* possible to prepare for an oral interview – in several ways:

1) Keep a copy of your application and review it carefully before the interview

This may be the only document before the oral board, and the starting point of the interview. Know what education and experience you have listed there, and the sequence and dates of all of it. Sometimes the board will ask you to review the highlights of your experience for them; you should not have to hem and haw doing it.

2) Study the class specification and the examination announcement

Usually, the oral board has one or both of these to guide them. The qualities, characteristics or knowledges required by the position sought are stated in these documents. They offer valuable clues as to the nature of the oral interview. For example, if the job involves supervisory responsibilities, the announcement will usually indicate that knowledge of modern supervisory methods and the qualifications of the candidate as a supervisor will be tested. If so, you can expect such questions, frequently in the form of a hypothetical situation which you are expected to solve. NEVER go into an oral without knowledge of the duties and responsibilities of the job you seek.

3) Think through each qualification required

Try to visualize the kind of questions you would ask if you were a board member. How well could you answer them? Try especially to appraise your own knowledge and background in each area, *measured against the job sought*, and identify any areas in which you are weak. Be critical and realistic – do not flatter yourself.

4) Do some general reading in areas in which you feel you may be weak

For example, if the job involves supervision and your past experience has NOT, some general reading in supervisory methods and practices, particularly in the field of human relations, might be useful. Do NOT study agency procedures or detailed manuals. The oral board will be testing your understanding and capacity, not your memory.

5) Get a good night's sleep and watch your general health and mental attitude

You will want a clear head at the interview. Take care of a cold or any other minor ailment, and of course, no hangovers.

What should be done on the day of the interview?

Now comes the day of the interview itself. Give yourself plenty of time to get there. Plan to arrive somewhat ahead of the scheduled time, particularly if your appointment is in the fore part of the day. If a previous candidate fails to appear, the board might be ready for you a bit early. By early afternoon an oral board is almost invariably behind schedule if there are many candidates, and you may have to wait.

Take along a book or magazine to read, or your application to review, but leave any extraneous material in the waiting room when you go in for your interview. In any event, relax and compose yourself.

The matter of dress is important. The board is forming impressions about you – from your experience, your manners, your attitude, and your appearance. Give your personal appearance careful attention. Dress your best, but not your flashiest. Choose conservative, appropriate clothing, and be sure it is immaculate. This is a business interview, and your appearance should indicate that you regard it as such. Besides, being well groomed and properly dressed will help boost your confidence.

Sooner or later, someone will call your name and escort you into the interview room. *This is it.* From here on you are on your own. It is too late for any more preparation. But remember, you asked for this opportunity to prove your fitness, and you are here because your request was granted.

What happens when you go in?

The usual sequence of events will be as follows: The clerk (who is often the board stenographer) will introduce you to the chairman of the oral board, who will introduce you to the other members of the board. Acknowledge the introductions before you sit down. Do not be surprised if you find a microphone facing you or a stenotypist sitting by. Oral interviews are usually recorded in the event of an appeal or other review.

Usually the chairman of the board will open the interview by reviewing the highlights of your education and work experience from your application – primarily for the benefit of the other members of the board, as well as to get the material into the record. Do not interrupt or comment unless there is an error or significant misinterpretation; if that is the case, do not hesitate. But do not quibble about insignificant matters. Also, he will usually ask you some question about your education, experience or your present job – partly to get you to start talking and to establish the interviewing "rapport." He may start the actual questioning, or turn it over to one of the other members. Frequently, each member undertakes the questioning on a particular area, one in which he is perhaps most competent, so you can expect each member to participate in the examination. Because time is limited, you may also expect some rather abrupt switches in the direction the questioning takes, so do not be upset by it. Normally, a board member will not pursue a single line of questioning unless he discovers a particular strength or weakness.

After each member has participated, the chairman will usually ask whether any member has any further questions, then will ask you if you have anything you wish to add. Unless you are expecting this question, it may floor you. Worse, it may start you off on an extended, extemporaneous speech. The board is not usually seeking more information. The question is principally to offer you a last opportunity to present further qualifications or to indicate that you have nothing to add. So, if you feel that a significant qualification or characteristic has been overlooked, it is proper to point it out in a sentence or so. Do not compliment the board on the thoroughness of their examination – they have been sketchy, and you know it. If you wish, merely say, "No thank you, I have nothing further to add." This is a point where you can "talk yourself out" of a good impression or fail to present an important bit of information. Remember, *you close the interview yourself.*

The chairman will then say, "That is all, Mr. _____, thank you." Do not be startled; the interview is over, and quicker than you think. Thank him, gather your belongings and take your leave. Save your sigh of relief for the other side of the door.

How to put your best foot forward

Throughout this entire process, you may feel that the board individually and collectively is trying to pierce your defenses, seek out your hidden weaknesses and embarrass and confuse you. Actually, this is not true. They are obliged to make an appraisal of your qualifications for the job you are seeking, and they want to see you in your best light. Remember, they must interview all candidates and a non-cooperative candidate may become a failure in spite of their best efforts to bring out his qualifications. Here are 15 suggestions that will help you:

1) Be natural – Keep your attitude confident, not cocky

If you are not confident that you can do the job, do not expect the board to be. Do not apologize for your weaknesses, try to bring out your strong points. The board is interested in a positive, not negative, presentation. Cockiness will antagonize any board member and make him wonder if you are covering up a weakness by a false show of strength.

2) Get comfortable, but don't lounge or sprawl

Sit erectly but not stiffly. A careless posture may lead the board to conclude that you are careless in other things, or at least that you are not impressed by the importance of the occasion. Either conclusion is natural, even if incorrect. Do not fuss with your clothing, a pencil or an ashtray. Your hands may occasionally be useful to emphasize a point; do not let them become a point of distraction.

3) Do not wisecrack or make small talk

This is a serious situation, and your attitude should show that you consider it as such. Further, the time of the board is limited – they do not want to waste it, and neither should you.

4) Do not exaggerate your experience or abilities

In the first place, from information in the application or other interviews and sources, the board may know more about you than you think. Secondly, you probably will not get away with it. An experienced board is rather adept at spotting such a situation, so do not take the chance.

5) If you know a board member, do not make a point of it, yet do not hide it

Certainly you are not fooling him, and probably not the other members of the board. Do not try to take advantage of your acquaintanceship – it will probably do you little good.

6) Do not dominate the interview

Let the board do that. They will give you the clues – do not assume that you have to do all the talking. Realize that the board has a number of questions to ask you, and do not try to take up all the interview time by showing off your extensive knowledge of the answer to the first one.

7) Be attentive

You only have 20 minutes or so, and you should keep your attention at its sharpest throughout. When a member is addressing a problem or question to you, give him your undivided attention. Address your reply principally to him, but do not exclude the other board members.

8) Do not interrupt

A board member may be stating a problem for you to analyze. He will ask you a question when the time comes. Let him state the problem, and wait for the question.

9) Make sure you understand the question

Do not try to answer until you are sure what the question is. If it is not clear, restate it in your own words or ask the board member to clarify it for you. However, do not haggle about minor elements.

10) Reply promptly but not hastily

A common entry on oral board rating sheets is "candidate responded readily," or "candidate hesitated in replies." Respond as promptly and quickly as you can, but do not jump to a hasty, ill-considered answer.

11) Do not be peremptory in your answers

A brief answer is proper – but do not fire your answer back. That is a losing game from your point of view. The board member can probably ask questions much faster than you can answer them.

12) Do not try to create the answer you think the board member wants

He is interested in what kind of mind you have and how it works – not in playing games. Furthermore, he can usually spot this practice and will actually grade you down on it.

13) Do not switch sides in your reply merely to agree with a board member

Frequently, a member will take a contrary position merely to draw you out and to see if you are willing and able to defend your point of view. Do not start a debate, yet do not surrender a good position. If a position is worth taking, it is worth defending.

14) Do not be afraid to admit an error in judgment if you are shown to be wrong

The board knows that you are forced to reply without any opportunity for careful consideration. Your answer may be demonstrably wrong. If so, admit it and get on with the interview.

15) Do not dwell at length on your present job

The opening question may relate to your present assignment. Answer the question but do not go into an extended discussion. You are being examined for a *new* job, not your present one. As a matter of fact, try to phrase ALL your answers in terms of the job for which you are being examined.

Basis of Rating

Probably you will forget most of these "do's" and "don'ts" when you walk into the oral interview room. Even remembering them all will not ensure you a passing grade. Perhaps you did not have the qualifications in the first place. But remembering them will help you to put your best foot forward, without treading on the toes of the board members.

Rumor and popular opinion to the contrary notwithstanding, an oral board wants you to make the best appearance possible. They know you are under pressure – but they also want to see how you respond to it as a guide to what your reaction would be under the pressures of the job you seek. They will be influenced by the degree of poise you display, the personal traits you show and the manner in which you respond.

EXAMINATION SECTION

Directions: Each question or incomplete statement is followed by several suggested answers or completions. Select the one that BEST answers the question or completes the statement. *PRINT THE LETTER OF THE CORRECT ANSWER IN THE SPACE AT THE RIGHT.*

Questions 1-9.

DIRECTIONS: In questions 1-9, you will read a set of facts and a conclusion drawn from them. The conclusion may be valid or invalid, based on the facts—it's your task to determine the validity of the conclusion.

For each question, select the letter before the statement that BEST expresses the relationship between the given facts and the conclusion that has been drawn from them. Your choices are:

     A.   The facts prove the conclusion
     B.   The facts disprove the conclusion; or
     C.   The facts neither prove nor disprove the conclusion.

1)   FACTS: Lauren must use Highway 29 to get to work. Lauren has a meeting today at 9:00 am. If she misses the meeting, Lauren will probably lose a major account. Highway 29 is closed all day today for repairs.

1. _____

CONCLUSION: Lauren will not be able to get to work.

A.   The facts prove the conclusion.
B.   The facts disprove the conclusion.
C.   The facts neither prove nor disprove the conclusion.

2)   FACTS: The Tumbleweed Follies, a traveling burlesque show, is looking for a new line dancer. The position requires both singing and dancing skills. If the show cannot fill the position by Friday, it will begin to look for a magician to fill the time slot currently held by the line dancers. Willa, who wants to audition for the line dancing position, can sing, but cannot dance.

2. _____

CONCLUSION: Willa is qualified to audition for the part of line dancer.

A.   The facts prove the conclusion.
B.   The facts disprove the conclusion.
C.   The facts neither prove nor disprove the conclusion.

3)   FACTS: Terry owns two dogs, Spike and Stan. One of the dogs is short-haired and has blue eyes. One dog has a pink nose. The blue-eyed dog never barks. One of the dogs has white fur on its paws. Sam has long hair.

3. _____

CONCLUSION: Spike never barks.

A.   The facts prove the conclusion.
B.   The facts disprove the conclusion.
C.   The facts neither prove nor disprove the conclusion.

4)   FACTS: No science teachers are members of the PTA. Some English teachers are members of the PTA. Some English teachers in the PTA also wear glasses. Every PTA member is required to sit on the dunking stool at the student carnival except for those who wear glasses, who will be exempt. Those who are exempt, however, will have to officiate the hamster races. All of the English teachers in the PTA who do not wear glasses are married.

4. _____

CONCLUSION: All the married English teachers in the PTA will sit on the dunking stool at the student carnival.

A.   The facts prove the conclusion.
B.   The facts disprove the conclusion.
C.   The facts neither prove nor disprove the conclusion.

5)   FACTS: If the price of fuel is increased and sales remain constant, oil company profits will increase. The price of fuel was increased, and market experts project that sales levels are likely to be maintained.

5. _____

CONCLUSION: The price of fuel will increase.

A.   The facts prove the conclusion.
B.   The facts disprove the conclusion.
C.   The facts neither prove nor disprove the conclusion.

6)   FACTS: Some members of the gymnastics team are double-jointed, and some members of the gymnastics team are also on the lacrosse team. Some double-jointed members of the gymnastics team are also coaches. All gymnastics team members perform floor exercises, except the coaches. All the double-jointed members of the gymnastics team who are not coaches are freshmen.

6. _____

CONCLUSION: Some double-jointed freshmen are coaches.

A.   The facts prove the conclusion.
B.   The facts disprove the conclusion.
C.   The facts neither prove nor disprove the conclusion.

7)   FACTS: Each member of the International Society speaks at least one   7. _____
foreign language, but no member speaks more than four foreign languages.
Five members speak Spanish; three speak Mandarin; four speak French; four
speak German; and five speak a foreign language other than Spanish, Mandarin, French, or German.

CONCLUSION: The lowest possible number of members in the International
Society is eight.

A.   The facts prove the conclusion.
B.   The facts disprove the conclusion.
C.   The facts neither prove nor disprove the conclusion.

8)   FACTS: Mary keeps seven cats in her apartment. Only three of the   8. _____
cats will eat the same kind of food. Mary wants to keep at least one extra bag
of each kind of food.

CONCLUSION: The minimum number of bags Mary will need to keep as
extra is 7.

A.   The facts prove the conclusion.
B.   The facts disprove the conclusion.
C.   The facts neither prove nor disprove the conclusion.

9)   FACTS: In Ed and Marie's exercise group, everyone likes the treadmill   9. _____
or the stationary bicycle, or both, but Ed does not like the stationary bicycle.
Marie has not expressed a preference, but spends most of her time on the stationary bicycle.

CONCLUSION: Everyone in the group who does not like the treadmill likes
the stationary bicycle.

A.   The facts prove the conclusion.
B.   The facts disprove the conclusion.
C.   The facts neither prove nor disprove the conclusion.

Questions 10-17.

DIRECTIONS: Questions 10-17 are based on the following reading passage. It is not your knowledge of the particular topic that is being tested, but your ability to reason based on what you have read. The passage is likely to detail several proposed courses of action and factors affecting these proposals. The reading passage is followed by a conclusion or outcome based on the facts in the passage, or a description of a decision taken regarding the situation. The conclusion is followed by a number of statements that have a possible connection to the conclusion. For each statement, you are to determine whether:

    A.   The statement proves the conclusion.
    B.   The statement supports the conclusion but does not prove it.
    C.   The statement disproves the conclusion.
    D.   The statement weakens the conclusion but does not disprove it.
    E.   The statement has no relevance to the conclusion.

Remember that the conclusion after the passage is to be accepted as the outcome of what actually happened, and that you are being asked to evaluate the impact each statement would have had on the conclusion.

PASSAGE:

The Owyhee Mission School District's Board of Directors is hosting a public meeting to debate the merits of the proposed abolition of all bilingual education programs within the district. The group that has made the proposal believes the programs, which teach immigrant children academic subjects in their native language until they have learned English well enough to join mainstream classes, inhibit the ability of students to acquire English quickly and succeed in school and in the larger American society. Such programs, they argue, are also a wasteful drain on the district's already scant resources.

At the meeting, several teachers and parents stand to speak out against the proposal. The purpose of an education, they say, should be to build upon, rather than dismantle, a minority child's language and culture. By teaching children in academic subjects in their native tongues, while simultaneously offering English language instruction, schools can meet the goals of learning English and progressing through academic subjects along with their peers.

Hiram Nguyen, a representative of the parents whose children are currently enrolled in bilingual education, stands at the meeting to express the parents' wishes. The parents have been polled, he says, and are overwhelmingly of the opinion that while language and culture are important to them, they are not things that will disappear from the students' lives if they are no longer taught in the classroom. The most important issue for the parents is whether their children will succeed in school and be competitive in the larger American society. If bilingual education can be demonstrated to do that, then the parents are in favor of continuing it.

At the end of the meeting, a proponent of the plan, Oscar Ramos, stands to clarify some misconceptions about the proposal. It does not call for a "sink or swim" approach, he says, but allows for an interpreter to be present in mainstream classes to explain anything a student finds too complex or confusing.

The last word of the meeting is given to Delia Cruz, a bilingual teacher at one of the district's elementary schools. A student is bound to find anything complex or confusing, she says, if it is spoken in a language he has never heard before. It is more wasteful to place children in classrooms where they don't understand anything, she says, than it is to try to teach them something useful as they are learning the English language.

CONCLUSION: After the meeting, the Owyhee Mission School District's Board of Directors votes to terminate all the district's bilingual education programs at the end of the current academic year, but to maintain the current level of funding to each of the schools that have programs cut.

10)   A poll conducted by the *Los Angeles Times* at approximately the same time as the Board's meeting indicated that 75% of the people were opposed to bilingual education; among Latinos, opposition was 84%.

10. _____

A.

B.

C.

D.

E.

11)   Of all the studies conducted on bilingual education programs, 64% indicate that students learned English grammar better in "sink or swim" classes without any special features than they did in bilingual education classes.

11. _____

A.

B.

C.

D.

E.

12)   In the academic year that begins after the Board's vote, Montgomery Burns Elementary, an Owyhee Mission District school, launches a new bilingual program for the children of Somali immigrants.

12. _____

A.

B.

C.

D.

E.

13)   In the previous academic year, under severe budget restraints, the Ow-   13. _____
yhee Mission District cut all physical education, music, and art classes, but its
funding for bilingual education classes increased by 18%.

A.
B.
C.
D.
E.

14)   Before the Board votes, a polling consultant conducts randomly   14. _____
sampled assessments of immigrant students who enrolled in Owyhee district
schools at a time when they did not speak any English at all. Ten years after
graduating from high school, 44% of those who received bilingual instruction
were professionals—doctors, lawyers, educators, engineers, etc. Of those who
did not receive bilingual education, 38% were professionals.

A.
B.
C.
D.
E.

15)   Over the past several years, the scores of Owyhee District students   15. _____
have gradually declined, and enrollment numbers have followed as anxious
parents transferred their children to other schools or applied for a state-funded
voucher program.

A.
B.
C.
D.
E.

16)   California and Massachusetts, two of the most liberal states in the   16. _____
country, have each passed ballot measures banning bilingual education in public schools.

A.
B.
C.
D.
E.

17) In the academic year that begins after the Board's vote, no Owyhee Mission District Schools are conducting bilingual instruction.

17. _____

A.
B.
C.
D.
E.

Questions 18-25.

DIRECTIONS: Questions 18-25 each provide four factual statements and a conclusion based on these statements. After reading the entire question, you will decide whether:

A.   The conclusion is proved by statements 1-4;
B.   The conclusion is disproved by statements 1-4; or
C.   The facts are not sufficient to prove or disprove the conclusion.

18) FACTUAL STATEMENTS:

18. _____

1.   Gear X rotates in a clockwise direction if Switch C is in the OFF position
2.   Gear X will rotate in a counter-clockwise direction if Switch C is ON.
3.   If Gear X is rotating in a clockwise direction, then Gear Y will not be rotating at all.
4.   Switch C is OFF.

CONCLUSION: Gear Y is rotating.

A.   The conclusion is proved by statements 1-4.
B.   The conclusion is disproved by statements 1-4.
C.   The facts are not sufficient to prove or disprove the conclusion.

19) FACTUAL STATEMENTS:

19. _____

1.   Mark is older than Jim but younger than Dan.
2.   Fern is older than Mark but younger than Silas.
3.   Dan is younger than Silas but older than Edward.
4.   Edward is older than Mark but younger than Fern.

CONCLUSION: Dan is older than Fern.

A.   The conclusion is proved by statements 1-4.
B.   The conclusion is disproved by statements 1-4.
C.   The facts are not sufficient to prove or disprove the conclusion.

20) FACTUAL STATEMENTS: 20. _____

1. Each of Fred's three sofa cushions lies on top of four lost coins.
2. The cushion on the right covers two pennies and two dimes.
3. The middle cushion covers two dimes and two quarters.
4. The cushion on the left covers two nickels and two quarters.

CONCLUSION: To be guaranteed of retrieving at least one coin of each
denomination, and without looking at any of the coins, Frank must take three
coins each from under the cushions on the right and the left.

A. The conclusion is proved by statements 1-4.
B. The conclusion is disproved by statements 1-4.
C. The facts are not sufficient to prove or disprove the conclusion.

21) FACTUAL STATEMENTS: 21. _____

1. The door to the hammer mill chamber is locked if light 6 is red.
2. The door to the hammer mill chamber is locked only when the mill is
operating.
3. If the mill is not operating, light 6 is blue.
4. The door to the hammer mill chamber is locked.

CONCLUSION: The mill is in operation.

A. The conclusion is proved by statements 1-4.
B. The conclusion is disproved by statements 1-4.
C. The facts are not sufficient to prove or disprove the conclusion.

22) FACTUAL STATEMENTS: 22. _____

1. In a five-story office building, where each story is occupied by a single
professional, Dr. Kane's office is above Dr. Assad's.
2. Dr. Johnson's office is between Dr. Kane's and Dr. Conlon's.
3. Dr. Steen's office is between Dr. Conlon's and Dr. Assad's.
4. Dr. Johnson is on the fourth story.

CONCLUSION: Dr. Steen occupies the second story.

A. The conclusion is proved by statements 1-4.
B. The conclusion is disproved by statements 1-4.
C. The facts are not sufficient to prove or disprove the conclusion.

23) FACTUAL STATEMENTS: 23. _____

1.   On Saturday, farmers Hank, Earl, Roy, and Cletus plowed a total of 520 acres.
2.   Hank plowed twice as many acres as Roy.
3.   Roy plowed half as much as the farmer who plowed the most.
4.   Cletus plowed 160 acres.

CONCLUSION: Hank plowed 200 acres.

A.   The conclusion is proved by statements 1-4.
B.   The conclusion is disproved by statements 1-4.
C.   The facts are not sufficient to prove or disprove the conclusion.

24) FACTUAL STATEMENTS: 24. _____

1.   Four travelers—Tina, Jodie, Alex, and Oscar—each traveled to a different island—Aruba, Jamaica, Nevis, and Barbados—but not necessarily respectively.
2.   Tina did not travel as far to Jamaica as Jodie traveled to her island.
3.   Oscar traveled twice as far as Alex, who traveled the same distance as the traveler who went to Aruba.
4.   Oscar went to Barbados.

CONCLUSION: Oscar traveled the farthest.

A.   The conclusion is proved by statements 1-4.
B.   The conclusion is disproved by statements 1-4.
C.   The facts are not sufficient to prove or disprove the conclusion.

25) FACTUAL STATEMENTS: 25. _____

1.   In the natural history museum, every Native American display that contains pottery also contains beadwork.
2.   Some of the displays containing lodge replicas also contain beadwork.
3.   The display on the Choctaw, a Native American tribe, contains pottery.
4.   The display on the Modoc, a Native American tribe, contains only two of these items.

CONCLUSION: If the Modoc display contains pottery, it does not contain lodge replicas.

A.   The conclusion is proved by statements 1-4.
B.   The conclusion is disproved by statements 1-4.
C.   The facts are not sufficient to prove or disprove the conclusion.

KEY (CORRECT ANSWERS)

1. A
2. B
3. A
4. A
5. C

6. B
7. B
8. B
9. A
10. B

11. B
12. C
13. B
14. D
15. E

16. E
17. A
18. B
19. C
20. A

21. A
22. A
23. C
24. A
25. A

TEST 2

Directions: Each question or incomplete statement is followed by several suggested answers or completions. Select the one that BEST answers the question or completes the statement. *PRINT THE LETTER OF THE CORRECT ANSWER IN THE SPACE AT THE RIGHT.*

Questions 1-9.

DIRECTIONS: In questions 1-9, you will read a set of facts and a conclusion drawn from them. The conclusion may be valid or invalid, based on the facts—it's your task to determine the validity of the conclusion.

For each question, select the letter before the statement that BEST expresses the relationship between the given facts and the conclusion that has been drawn from them. Your choices are:

     A.   The facts prove the conclusion
     B.   The facts disprove the conclusion; or
     C.   The facts neither prove nor disprove the conclusion.

1)   FACTS: If the maximum allowable income for Medicaid recipients is increased, the number of Medicaid recipients will increase. If the number of Medicaid recipients increases, more funds must be allocated to the Medicaid program, which will require a tax increase. Taxes cannot be approved without the approval of the legislature. The legislature probably will not approve a tax increase.

CONCLUSION: The maximum allowable income for Medicaid recipients will increase.

A.   The facts prove the conclusion.
B.   The facts disprove the conclusion.
C.   The facts neither prove nor disprove the conclusion.

1. _____

2)   FACTS: All the dentists on the baseball team are short. Everyone in the dugout is a dentist, but not everyone in the dugout is short. The baseball team is not made up of people of any particular profession.

CONCLUSION: Some people who are not dentists are in the dugout.

A.   The facts prove the conclusion.
B.   The facts disprove the conclusion.
C.   The facts neither prove nor disprove the conclusion.

2. _____

3)   FACTS: A taxi company's fleet is divided into two fleets. Fleet One   3. _____
contains cabs A, B, C, and D. Fleet Two contains E, F, G, and H. Each cab is
either yellow or green. Five of the cabs are yellow. Cabs A and E are not both
yellow. Either Cab C or F, or both, are not yellow. Cabs B and H are either
both yellow or both green.

CONCLUSION: Cab H is green.

A.   The facts prove the conclusion.
B.   The facts disprove the conclusion.
C.   The facts neither prove nor disprove the conclusion.

4)   FACTS: Most people in the skydiving club are not afraid of heights.   4. _____
Everyone in the skydiving club makes three parachute jumps a month.

CONCLUSION: At least one person who is afraid of heights makes three
parachute jumps a month.

A.   The facts prove the conclusion.
B.   The facts disprove the conclusion.
C.   The facts neither prove nor disprove the conclusion.

5)   FACTS: If the Board approves the new rule, the agency will move to a   5. _____
new location immediately. If the agency moves, five new supervisors will be
immediately appointed. The Board has approved the new proposal.

CONCLUSION: No new supervisors were appointed.

A.   The facts prove the conclusion.
B.   The facts disprove the conclusion.
C.   The facts neither prove nor disprove the conclusion.

6)   FACTS: All the workers at the supermarket chew gum when they sack   6. _____
groceries. Sometimes Lance, a supermarket worker, doesn't chew gum at all
when he works. Another supermarket worker, Jenny, chews gum the whole
time she is at work.

CONCLUSION: Jenny always sacks groceries when she is at work.

A.   The facts prove the conclusion.
B.   The facts disprove the conclusion.
C.   The facts neither prove nor disprove the conclusion.

7)   FACTS: Lake Lottawatta is bigger than Lake Tacomi. Lake Tacomi
and Lake Ottawa are exactly the same size. All lakes in Montana are bigger
than Lake Ottawa.

CONCLUSION: Lake Lottawatta is in Montana.

A.   The facts prove the conclusion.
B.   The facts disprove the conclusion.
C.   The facts neither prove nor disprove the conclusion.

7. _____

8)   FACTS: Two men, Cox and Taylor, are playing poker at a table. Taylor has a pair of aces in his hand. One man is smoking a cigar. One of them
has no pairs in his hand and is wearing an eye patch. The man wearing the
eye patch is smoking a cigar. One man is bald.

CONCLUSION: Cox is smoking a cigar.

A.   The facts prove the conclusion.
B.   The facts disprove the conclusion.
C.   The facts neither prove nor disprove the conclusion.

8. _____

9)   FACTS: All Kwakiutls are Wakashan Indians. All Wakashan Indians
originated on Vancouver Island. The Nootka also originated on Vancouver
Island.

CONCLUSION: Kwakiutls originated on Vancouver Island.

A.   The facts prove the conclusion.
B.   The facts disprove the conclusion.
C.   The facts neither prove nor disprove the conclusion.

9. _____

Questions 10-17.

DIRECTIONS: Questions 10-17 are based on the following reading passage.
It is not your knowledge of the particular topic that is being tested, but your
ability to reason based on what you have read. The passage is likely to detail
several proposed courses of action and factors affecting these proposals. The
reading passage is followed by a conclusion or outcome based on the facts in
the passage, or a description of a decision taken regarding the situation. The
conclusion is followed by a number of statements that have a possible connection to the conclusion. For each statement, you are to determine whether:

    A.   The statement proves the conclusion.
    B.   The statement supports the conclusion but does not prove it.
    C.   The statement disproves the conclusion.
    D.   The statement weakens the conclusion but does not disprove it.
    E.   The statement has no relevance to the conclusion.

Remember that the conclusion after the passage is to be accepted as the outcome of what actually happened, and that you are being asked to evaluate the
impact each statement would have had on the conclusion.

PASSAGE:

     The World Wide Web portal and search engine. HipBot, is considering
becoming a subscription-only service, locking out nonsubscribers from the
content on its Web site. HipBot currently relies solely on advertising revenues.
     HipBot's content director says that by taking in an annual fee from
each customer, the company can both increase profits and provide premium
content that no other portal can match.
     The marketing director disagrees, saying that there is no guarantee that
anyone who now visits the Web site for free will agree to pay for the privilege
of visiting it again. Most will probably simply use of the other major portals.
Also, HipBot's advertising clients will not be happy when they learn that the
site will be viewed by a more limited number of people.

CONCLUSION: In January of 2010, the CEO of HipBot decides to keep the
portal open to all Web users, with some limited "premium content" available
to subscribers who don't mind paying a little extra to access it. The company
will aim to maintain, or perhaps increase, its advertising revenue.

10)   In an independent marketing survey, 62% of respondents said they
"strongly agree" with the following statement: "I almost never pay attention to
advertisements that appear on the World Wide Web."

A.
B.
C.
D.
E.

11)   When it learns about the subscription-only debate going on at HipBot,
Wernham Hogg Entertainment, one of HipBot's most reliable clients, says it
will withdraw its ads and place them on a free Web portal if HipBot decides to
limit its content to subscribers. Wernham Hogg pays HipBot about $6 million
annually—about 12% of HipBot's gross revenues—to run its ads online.

A.
B.
C.
D.
E.

12)   At the end of the second quarter of FY 2010, after continued stagnant
profits, the CEO of HipBot assembles a blue ribbon commission to gather and
analyze data on the costs, benefits, and feasibility of adding a limited amount
of "premium" content to the HipBot portal.

A.
B.
C.
D.
E.

13)   In the following fiscal year, Wernham Hogg Entertainment, satisfied
with the "hit counts" on HipBot's free Web site, spends another $1 million on
advertisements that will appear on Web pages that are available to HipBot's
"premium" subscribers.

A.
B.
C.
D.
E.

14) HipBot's information technology director reports that the engineers in his department have come up with a feature that will search not only individual web pages, but tie into other Web-based search engines, as well, and then comb through all these results to find those most relevant to the user's search.

14. _____

A.
B.
C.
D.
E.

15) In an independent marketing survey, 79% of respondents said they "strongly agree" with the following statement: "Many Web sites are so dominated by advertisements these days that it is increasingly frustrating to find the content I want to read or see."

15. _____

A.
B.
C.
D.
E.

16) After three years of studies at the federal level, the Department of Commerce releases a report suggesting that in general, the only private "subscriber-only" Web sites that do well financially are those with a very specialized user population.

16. _____

A.
B.
C.
D.
E.

17) HipBot's own marketing research indicates that the introduction of premium content has the potential to attract new users to the HipBot portal.

17. _____

A.
B.
C.
D.
E.

Questions 18-25.

DIRECTIONS: Questions 18-25 each provide four factual statements and a conclusion based on these statements. After reading the entire question, you will decide whether:

    A.   The conclusion is proved by statements 1-4;
    B.   The conclusion is disproved by statements 1-4; or
    C.   The facts are not sufficient to prove or disprove the conclusion.

18)   FACTUAL STATEMENTS: 18. _____

1.   If the alarm goes off, Sam will wake up.
2.   If Tandy wakes up before 4:00, Linda will leave the bedroom and sleep on the couch.
3.   If Linda leaves the bedroom, she'll check the alarm to make sure it is working.
4.   The alarm goes off.

CONCLUSION: Tandy woke up before 4:00.

A.   The conclusion is proved by statements 1-4.
B.   The conclusion is disproved by statements 1-4.
C.   The facts are not sufficient to prove or disprove the conclusion.

19)   FACTUAL STATEMENTS: 19. _____

1.   Four brothers are named Earl, John, Gary, and Pete.
2.   Earl and Pete are unmarried.
3.   John is shorter than the youngest of the four.
4.   The oldest brother is married, and is also the tallest.

CONCLUSION: Pete is the youngest brother.

A.   The conclusion is proved by statements 1-4.
B.   The conclusion is disproved by statements 1-4.
C.   The facts are not sufficient to prove or disprove the conclusion.

20) FACTUAL STATEMENTS: 20. _____

1.   Automobile engines are cooled either by air or by liquid.
2.   If the engine is small and simple enough, air from a belt-driven fan will cool it sufficiently.
3.   Most newer automobile engines are too complicated to be air-cooled.
4.   Air-cooled engines are cheaper and easier to build than liquid-cooled engines.

CONCLUSION: Most newer automobile engines use liquid coolant.

A.   The conclusion is proved by statements 1-4.
B.   The conclusion is disproved by statements 1-4.
C.   The facts are not sufficient to prove or disprove the conclusion.

21) FACTUAL STATEMENTS: 21. _____

1.   Erica will only file a lawsuit if she is injured while parasailing.
2.   If Rick orders Trip to run a rope test, Trip will check the rigging.
3.   If the rigging does not malfunction, Erica will not be injured.
4.   Rick order Trip to run a rope test.

CONCLUSION: Erica does not file a lawsuit.

A.   The conclusion is proved by statements 1-4.
B.   The conclusion is disproved by statements 1-4.
C.   The facts are not sufficient to prove or disprove the conclusion.

22) FACTUAL STATEMENTS: 22. _____

1.   On Maple Street, which is four blocks long, Bill's shop is two blocks east of Ken's shop.
2.   Ken's shop is one block west of the only shop on Maple Street with an awning.
3.   Erma's shop is one block west of the easternmost block.
4.   Bill's shop is on the easternmost block.

CONCLUSION: Bill's shop has an awning.

A.   The conclusion is proved by statements 1-4.
B.   The conclusion is disproved by statements 1-4.
C.   The facts are not sufficient to prove or disprove the conclusion.

23)   FACTUAL STATEMENTS: 23. _____

1.   Gear X rotates in a clockwise direction if Switch C is in the OFF position

2.   Gear X will rotate in a counter-clockwise direction if Switch C is ON.

3.   If Gear X is rotating in a clockwise direction, then Gear Y will not be
rotating at all.

4.   Gear Y is rotating.

CONCLUSION: Gear X is rotating in a counter-clockwise direction.

A.   The conclusion is proved by statements 1-4.
B.   The conclusion is disproved by statements 1-4.
C.   The facts are not sufficient to prove or disprove the conclusion.

24)   FACTUAL STATEMENTS: 24. _____

1.   The Republic of Garbanzo's currency system has four basic denominations: the pastor, the noble, the donner, and the rojo.

2.   A pastor is worth 2 nobles.

3.   2 donners can be exchanged for a rojo.

4.   3 pastors are equal in value to 2 donners.

CONCLUSION: The rojo is most valuable.

A.   The conclusion is proved by statements 1-4.
B.   The conclusion is disproved by statements 1-4.
C.   The facts are not sufficient to prove or disprove the conclusion.

25)   FACTUAL STATEMENTS: 25. _____

1.   At Prickett's Nursery, the only citrus trees left are either Meyer lemons
or Valencia oranges, and every citrus tree left is either a dwarf or a semidwarf.

2.   Half of the semidwarf trees are Meyer lemons.

3.   There are more semidwarf trees left than dwarf trees.

4.   A quarter of the dwarf trees are Valencia oranges.

CONCLUSION: There are more Valencia oranges left at Prickett's Nursery
than Meyer lemons.

A.   The conclusion is proved by statements 1-4.
B.   The conclusion is disproved by statements 1-4.
C.   The facts are not sufficient to prove or disprove the conclusion.

KEY (CORRECT ANSWERS)

1. C
2. B
3. B
4. A
5. B

6. C
7. C
8. A
9. A
10. E

11. B
12. C
13. A
14. E
15. D

16. B
17. B
18. C
19. C
20. A

21. C
22. B
23. C
24. A
25. B

EXAMINATION SECTION
TEST 1

Directions: Each question or incomplete statement is followed by several suggested answers or completions. Select the one that BEST answers the question or completes the statement. *PRINT THE LETTER OF THE CORRECT ANSWER IN THE SPACE AT THE RIGHT.*

1) When conducting a needs assessment for the purpose of education planning, an agency's FIRST step is to identify or provide

    A. a profile of population characteristics
    B. barriers to participation
    C. existing resources
    D. profiles of competing resources

1. _____

2) Research has demonstrated that of the following, the most effective medium for communicating with external publics is/are

    A. video news releases
    B. television
    C. radio
    D. newspapers

2. _____

3) Basic ideas behind the effort to influence the attitudes and behaviors of a constituency include each of the following, EXCEPT the idea that

    A. words, rather than actions or events, are most likely to motivate
    B. demands for action are a usual response
    C. self-interest usually figures heavily into public involvement
    D. the reliability of change programs is difficult to assess

3. _____

4) An agency representative is trying to craft a pithy message to constituents in order to encourage the use agency program resources. Choosing an audience for such messages is easiest when the message

    A. is project- or behavior-based
    B. is combined with other messages
    C. is abstract
    D. has a broad appeal

4. _____

5) Of the following factors, the most important to the success of an agency's external education or communication programs is the

    5._____

A. amount of resources used to implement them
B. public's prior experiences with the agency
C. real value of the program to the public
D. commitment of the internal audience

6) A representative for a state agency is being interviewed by a reporter from a local news network. The representative is being asked to defend a program that is extremely unpopular in certain parts of the municipality. When a constituency is known to be opposed to a position, the most useful communication strategy is to present

    6._____

A. only the arguments that are consistent with constituents' views
B. only the agency's side of the issue
C. both sides of the argument as clearly as possible
D. both sides of the argument, omitting key information about the opposing position

7) The most significant barriers to effective agency community relations include

    7._____

    I. widespread distrust of communication strategies
    II. the media's "watchdog" stance
    III. public apathy
    IV. statutory opposition

A. I only
B. I and II
C. II and III
D. III and IV

8) In conducting an education program, many agencies use workshops and seminars in a classroom setting. Advantages of classroom-style teaching over other means of educating the public include each of the following, EXCEPT:

    8._____

A. enabling an instructor to verify learning through testing and interaction with the target audience
B. enabling hands-on practice and other participatory learning techniques
C. ability to reach an unlimited number of participants in a given length of time
D. ability to convey the latest, most up-to-date information

9) The _____ model of community relations is character-   9. _____
ized by an attempt to persuade the public to adopt the agency's point of view.

A.   two-way symmetric
B.   two-way asymmetric
C.   public information
D.   press agency/publicity

10)   Important elements of an internal situation analysis include the   10. _____

       I.   list of agency opponents
       II.   communication audit
       III.   updated organizational almanac
       IV.   stakeholder analysis

A.   I and II
B.   I, II and III
C.   II and III
D.   I, II, III and IV

11)   Government agency information efforts typically involve each of the   11. _____
following objectives, EXCEPT to

A.   implement changes in the policies of government agencies to align
with public opinion
B.   communicate the work of agencies
C.   explain agency techniques in a way that invites input from citizens
D.   provide citizen feedback to government administrators

12)   Factors that are likely to influence the effectiveness of an educational   12. _____
campaign include the

       I.   level of homogeneity among intended participants
       II.   number and types of media used
       III.   receptivity of the intended participants
       IV.   level of specificity in the message or behavior to be taught

A.   I and II
B.   I, II and III
C.   II and III
D.   I, II, III and IV

13)   An agency representative is writing instructional objectives that will   13. _____
later help to measure the effectiveness of an educational program. Which of
the following verbs, included in an objective, would be MOST helpful for the
purpose of measuring effectiveness?

A.   Know
B.   Identify
C.   Learn
D.   Comprehend

14)   A state education agency wants to encourage participation in a pro-   14. _____
gram that has just received a boost through new federal legislation. The program is intended to include participants from a wide variety of socioeconomic
and other demographic characteristics.
        The agency wants to launch a broad-based program that will inform
virtually every interested party in the state about the program's new circumstances. In attempting to deliver this message to such a wide-ranging constituency, the agency's best practice would be to

A.   broadcast the same message through as many different media channels
as possible
B.   focus on one discrete segment of the public at a time
C.   craft a message whose appeal is as broad as the public itself
D.   let the program's achievements speak for themselves and rely on word-
of-mouth

15)   Advantages associated with using the World Wide Web as an educa-   15. _____
tional tool include

        I.   an appeal to younger generations of the public
        II.   visually-oriented, interactive learning
        III.   learning that is not confined by space, time, or institutional as
               sociation
        IV.   a variety of methods for verifying use and learning

A.   I only
B.   I and II
C.   I, II and III
D.   I, II, III and IV

16)   In agencies involved in health care, community relations is a critical   16. _____
function because it

A.   serves as an intermediary between the agency and consumers
B.   generates a clear mission statement for agency goals and priorities
C.   ensures patient privacy while satisfying the media's right to informa-
tion
D.   helps marketing professionals determine the wants and needs of
agency constituents

17)   After an extensive campaign to promote its newest program to con-   17. _____
stituents, an agency learns that most of the audience did not understand the
intended message. Most likely, the agency has

A.   chosen words that were intended to inform, rather than persuade
B.   not accurately interpreted what the audience really needed to know
C.   overestimated the ability of the audience to receive and process the
message
D.   compensated for noise that may have interrupted the message

18)   The necessary elements that lead to conviction and motivation in the   18. _____
minds of participants in an educational or information program include each
of the following, EXCEPT the _____ of the message.

A.   acceptability
B.   intensity
C.   single-channel appeal
D.   pervasiveness

19)   Printed materials are often at the core of educational programs provid-   19. _____
ed by public agencies. The primary disadvantage associated with print is that
it

A.   does not enable comprehensive treatment of a topic
B.   is generally unreliable in term of assessing results
C.   is often the most expensive medium available
D.   is constrained by time

20)   Traditional thinking on public opinion holds that there is about ____   20. _____
_____ percent of the public who are pivotal to shifting the balance and mo-
mentum of opinion—they are concerned about an issue, but not fanatical, and
interested enough to pay attention to a reasoned discussion.

A.   2
B.   10
C.   33
D.   51

21)   One of the most useful guidelines for influencing attitude change   21. _____
among people is to

A.   inviting the target audience to come to you, rather than approaching
them
B.   use moral appeals as the primary approach
C.   use concrete images to enable people to see the results of behaviors or
indifference
D.   offer tangible rewards to people for changes in behaviors

22)   An agency is attempting to evaluate the effectiveness of its educational   22. _____
program. For this purpose, it wants to observe several focus groups discussing the same program. Which of the following would NOT be a guideline for
the use of focus groups?

A.   Focus groups should only include those who have participated in the
program.
B.   Be sure to accurately record the discussion.
C.   The same questions should be asked at each focus group meeting.
D.   It is often helpful to have a neutral, non-agency employee facilitate
discussions.

23)   Research consistently shows that _____ is the determinant   23. _____
most likely to make a newspaper editor run a news release.

A.   novelty
B.   prominence
C.   proximity
D.   conflict

24)   Which of the following is NOT one of the major variables to take into   24. _____
account when considering a population needs assessment?

A.   State of program development
B.   Resources available
C.   Demographics
D.   Community attitudes

25)   The first step in any communications audit is to   25. _____

A.   develop a research instrument
B.   determine how the organization currently communicates
C.   hire a contractor
D.   determine which audience to assess

KEY (CORRECT ANSWERS)

1. A
2. D
3. A
4. A
5. D

6. C
7. D
8. C
9. B
10. C

11. A
12. D
13. B
14. B
15. C

16. A
17. B
18. C
19. B
20. B

21. C
22. A
23. C
24. C
25. D

TEST 2

Directions: Each question or incomplete statement is followed by several suggested answers or completions. Select the one that BEST answers the question or completes the statement. *PRINT THE LETTER OF THE CORRECT ANSWER IN THE SPACE AT THE RIGHT.*

1) A public relations practitioner at an agency has just composed a press release highlighting a program's recent accomplishments and success stories. In pitching such releases to print outlets, the practitioner should

      I.   e-mail, mail, or send them by messenger
      II.   address them to "editor" or "news director"
      III.   have an assistant call all media contacts by telephone
      IV.   ask reporters or editors how they prefer to receive them

A.   I and II
B.   I and IV
C.   II, III and IV
D.   III only

1. _____

2) The "output goals" of an educational program are MOST likely to include

A.   specified ratings of services by participants on a standardized scale
B.   observable effects on a given community or clientele
C.   the number of instructional hours provided
D.   the number of participants served

2. _____

3) An agency wants to evaluate satisfaction levels among program participants, and mails out questionnaires to everyone who has been enrolled in the last year. The primary problem associated with this method of evaluative research is that it

A.   poses a significant inconvenience for respondents
B.   is inordinately expensive
C.   does not allow for follow-up or clarification questions
D.   usually involves a low response rate

3. _____

4) A communications audit is an important tool for measuring

A.   the depth of penetration of a particular message or program
B.   the cost of the organization's information campaigns
C.   how key audiences perceive an organization
D.   the commitment of internal stakeholders

4. _____

5) The "ABC's" of written learning objectives include each of the follow-   5. _____
ing, EXCEPT

A.   Audience
B.   Behavior
C.   Conditions
D.   Delineation

6) When attempting to change the behaviors of constituents, it is impor-   6. _____
tant to keep in mind that

    I.   most people are skeptical of communications that try to get
           them to change their behaviors
    II.   in most cases, a person selects the media to which he exposes
           himself
    III.   people tend to react defensively to messages or programs that
           rely on fear as a motivating factor
    IV.   programs should aim for the broadest appeal possible in order
           to include as many participants as possible

A.   I and II
B.   I, II and III
C.   II and III
D.   I, II, III and IV

7) The "laws" of public opinion include the idea that it is   7. _____

A.   useful for anticipating emergencies
B.   not sensitive to important events
C.   basically determined by self-interest
D.   sustainable through persistent appeals

8) Which of the following types of evaluations is used to measure public   8. _____
attitudes before and after an information/educational program?

A.   retrieval study
B.   copy test
C.   quota sampling
D.   benchmark study

9) The primary source for internal communications is/are usually   9. _____

A.   flow charts
B.   meetings
C.   voice mail
D.   printed publications

10)   An agency representative is putting together informational materials—   10. _____
brochures and a newsletter—outlining changes in one of the state's biggest
benefits programs. In assembling print materials as a medium for delivering
information to the public, the representative should keep in mind each of the
following trends:

    I.   For various reasons, the reading capabilities of the public are in
             general decline
    II.   Without tables and graphs to help illustrate the changes, it is
             unlikely that the message will be delivered effectively
    III.   Professionals and career-oriented people are highly receptive to
             information written in the form of a journal article or empirical
             study
    IV.   People tend to be put off by print materials that use itemized
             and bulleted (•) lists.

A.   I and II
B.   I, II and III
C.   II and III
D.   I, II, III and IV

11)   Which of the following steps in a problem-oriented information cam-   11. _____
paign would typically be implemented FIRST?

A.   Deciding on tactics
B.   Determining a communications strategy
C.   Evaluating the problem's impact
D.   Developing an organizational strategy

12)   A common pitfall in conducting an educational program is to   12. _____

A.   aim it at the wrong target audience
B.   overfund it
C.   leave it in the hands of people who are in the business of education,
rather than those with expertise in the business of the organization
D.   ignore the possibility that some other organization is meeting the same
educational need for the target audience

13)   The key factors that affect the credibility of an agency's educational   13. _____
program include

A.   organization
B.   scope
C.   sophistication
D.   penetration

14) Research on public opinion consistently demonstrates that it is 14. _____

A. easy to move people toward a strong opinion on anything, as long as they are approached directly through their emotions
B. easier to move people away from an opinion they currently hold than to have them form an opinion about something they have not previously cared about
C. easy to move people toward a strong opinion on anything, as long as the message appeals to their reason and intellect
D. difficult to move people toward a strong opinion on anything, no matter what the approach

15) In conducting an education program, many agencies use meetings and 15. _____ conferences to educate an audience about the organization and its programs. Advantages associated with this approach include

I. a captive audience that is known to be interested in the topic
II. ample opportunities for verifying learning
III. cost-efficient meeting space
IV. the ability to provide information on a wider variety of subjects

A. I and II
B. I, III and IV
C. II and III
D. I, II, III and IV

16) An agency is attempting to evaluate the effectiveness of its educational 16. _____ programs. For this purpose, it wants to observe several focus groups discussing particular programs. For this purpose, a focus group should never number more than _____ participants.

A. 5
B. 10
C. 15
D. 20

17) A _____ speech is written so that several agency members 17. _____ can deliver it to different audiences with only minor variations.

A. basic
B. printed
C. quota
D. pattern

18)   Which of the following statements about public opinion is generally   18. _____
considered to be FALSE?

A.   Opinion is primarily reactive rather than proactive.
B.   People have more opinions about goals than about the means by which
to achieve them.
C.   Facts tend to shift opinion in the accepted direction when opinion is
not solidly structured.
D.   Public opinion is based more on information than desire.

19)   An agency is trying to promote its educational program. As a general   19. _____
rule, the agency should NOT assume that

A.   people will only participate if they perceive an individual benefit
B.   promotions need to be aimed at small, discrete groups
C.   if the program is good, the audience will find out about it
D.   a variety of methods, including advertising, special events, and direct
mail, should be considered

20)   In planning a successful educational program, probably the first and   20. _____
most important question for an agency to ask is:

A.   What will be the content of the program?
B.   Who will be served by the program?
C.   When is the best time to schedule the program?
D.   Why is the program necessary?

21)   Media kits are LEAST likely to contain   21. _____

A.   fact sheets
B.   memoranda
C.   photographs with captions
D.   news releases

22)   The use of pamphlets and booklets as media for communication with   22. _____
the public often involves the disadvantage that

A.   the messages contained within them are frequently nonspecific
B.   it is difficult to measure their effectiveness in delivering the message
C.   there are few opportunities for people to refer to them
D.   color reproduction is poor

23) The most important prerequisite of a good educational program is an   23. _____

A. abundance of resources to implement it
B. individual staff unit formed for the purpose of program delivery
C. accurate needs assessment
D. uneducated constituency

24) After an education program has been delivered, an agency conducts a   24. _____
program evaluation to determine whether its objectives have been met. General rules about how to conduct such an education program evaluation include
each of the following, EXCEPT that it

A. must be done immediately after the program has been implemented
B. should be simple and easy to use
C. should be designed so that tabulation of responses can take place
quickly and inexpensively
D. should solicit mostly subjective, open-ended responses if the audience
was large

25) Using electronic media such as television as means of educating the   25. _____
public is typically recommended ONLY for agencies that

I. have a fairly simple message to begin with
II. want to reach the masses, rather than a targeted audience
III. have substantial financial resources
IV. accept that they will not be able to measure the results of the
campaign with much precision

A. I and II
B. I, II and III
C. II and IV
D. I, II, III and IV

KEY (CORRECT ANSWERS)

1. B
2. C
3. D
4. C
5. D

6. B
7. C
8. D
9. D
10. A

11. C
12. D
13. A
14. D
15. B

16. B
17. D
18. D
19. C
20. D

21. B
22. B
23. C
24. D
25. D

EXAMINATION SECTION

DIRECTIONS: Each question or incomplete statement is followed by several suggested answers or completions. Select the one that BEST answers the question or completes the statement. *PRINT THE LETTER OF THE CORRECT ANSWER IN THE SPACE AT THE RIGHT.*

1. Good procedure in handling complaints from the public may be divided into the following four principal stages:
   - I. Investigation of the complaint
   - II. Receipt of the complaint
   - III. Assignment of responsibility for investigation and correction
   - IV. Notification of correction

   The ORDER in which these stages ordinarily come is:
   - A. III, II, I, IV
   - B. II, III, I, IV
   - C. II, III, IV, I
   - D. II, IV, III, I

   1.____

2. The department may expect the MOST severe public criticism if
   - A. it asks for an increase in its annual budget
   - B. it purchases new and costly street cleaning equipment
   - C. sanitation officers and men are reclassified to higher salary grades
   - D. there is delay in cleaning streets of snow

   2.____

3. The MOST important function of public relations in the department should be to
   - A. develop cooperation on the part of the public in keeping streets clean
   - B. get stricter penalties enacted for health code violations
   - C. recruit candidates for entrance positions who can be developed into supervisors
   - D. train career personnel so that they can advance in the department

   3.____

4. The one of the following which has MOST frequently elicited unfavorable public comment has been
   - A. dirty sidewalks or streets
   - B. dumping on lots
   - C. failure to curb dogs
   - D. overflowing garbage cans

   4.____

5. It has been suggested that, as a public relations measure, sections hold *open house* for the public.
   The MOST effective time for this would be
   - A. during the summer when children are not in school and can accompany their parents
   - B. during the winter when snow is likely to fall and the public can see snow removal preparations

   5.__

C. immediately after a heavy snow storm when department snow removal operations are in full progress

D. when street sanitation is receiving general attention as during *Keep City Clean* week

6. When a public agency conducts a public relations program, it is MOST likely to find that each recipient of its message will

    A. disagree with the basic purpose of the message if the officials are not well known to him

    B. accept the message if it is presented by someone perceived as having a definite intention to persuade

    C. ignore the message unless it is presented in a literate and clever manner

    D. give greater attention to certain portions of the message as a result of his individual and cultural differences

6.___

7. Following are three statements about public relations and communications:

    I. A person who seeks to influence public opinion can speed up a trend

   II. Mass communications is the exposure of a mass audience to an idea

  III. All media are equally effective in reaching opinion leaders

Which of the following choices CORRECTLY classifies the above statements into those which are correct and those which are not?

    A. I and II are correct, but III is not

    B. II and III are correct, but I is not

    C. I and III are correct, but II is not

    D. III is correct, but I and II are not

7.___

8. Public relations experts say that MAXIMUM effect for a message results from

    A. concentrating in one medium

    B. ignoring mass media and concentrating on *opinion makers*

    C. presenting only those factors which support a given position

    D. using a combination of two or more of the available media

8.___

9. To assure credibility and avoid hostility, the public relations man MUST

    A. make certain his message is truthful, not evasive or exaggerated

    B. make sure his message contains some dire consequence if ignored

    C. repeat the message often enough so that it cannot be ignored

    D. try to reach as many people and groups as possible

9.___

10. The public relations man MUST be prepared to assume that members of his audience
    A. may have developed attitudes toward his proposals -- favorable, neutral, or unfavorable
    B. will be immediately hostile
    C. will consider his proposals with an open mind
    D. will invariably need an introduction to his subject

10.____

11. The one of the following statements that is CORRECT is:
    A. When a stupid question is asked of you by the public, it should be disregarded
    B. If you insist on formality between you and the public, the public will not be able to ask stupid questions that cannot be answered
    C. The public should be treated courteously, regardless of how stupid their questions may be
    D. You should explain to the public how stupid their questions are

11.____

12. With regard to public relations, the MOST important item which should be emphasized in an employee training program is that
    A. each inspector is a public relations agent
    B. an inspector should give the public all the information it asks for
    C. it is better to make mistakes and give erroneous information than to tell the public that you do not know the correct answer to their problem
    D. public relations is so specialized a field that only persons specially trained in it should consider it

12.____

13. Members of the public frequently ask about departmental procedures.
Of the following, it is BEST to
    A. advise the public to put the question in writing so that he can get a proper formal reply
    B. refuse to answer because this is a confidential matter
    C. explain the procedure as briefly as possible
    D. attempt to avoid the issue by discussing other matters

13.____

14. The effectiveness of a public relations program in a public agency such as the authority is BEST indicated by the
    A. amount of mass media publicity favorable to the policies of the authority
    B. morale of those employees who directly serve the patrons of the authority
    C. public's understanding and support of the authority's program and policies
    D. number of complaints received by the authority from patrons using its facilities

14.____

15. In an attempt to improve public opinion about a certain idea, the BEST course of action for an agency to take would be to present the
    A. clearest statements of the idea even though the language is somewhat technical

15.____

B. idea as the result of long-term studies
C. idea in association with something familiar to most people
D. idea as the viewpoint of the majority leaders

16. The fundamental factor in any agency's community relations program is

    16.__

    A. an outline of the objectives
    B. relations with the media
    C. the everyday actions of the employees
    D. a well-planned supervisory program

17. The FUNDAMENTAL factor in the success of a community relations program is

    17.__

    A. true commitment by the community
    B. true commitment by the administration
    C. a well-planned, systematic approach
    D. the actions of individuals in their contacts with the public

18. The statement below which is LEAST correct is:

    18.__

    A. Because of selection standards, the supervisor frequently encounters problems resulting from subordinates' inability to express themselves in the language of the profession
    B. Distortion of the meaning of a communication is usually brought about by a failure to use language that has a precise meaning to others
    C. The term *filtering* is the distortion or dilution of content of a communication that occurs as information is passed from individual to individual
    D. The complexity of the *communications net* will directly affect the speed and accuracy of messages flowing through it

19. Consider the following three statements that may or may not be CORRECT:

    19.__

    I. In order to prevent the stifling of communications flow, supervisors should insist that employees use the formal communications network
    II. Two-way communications are faster and more accurate than one-way communications
    III. There is a direct correlation between the effectiveness of communications and the total setting in which they occur

The choice below which MOST accurately describes the above statement is:

    A. All 3 are correct
    B. All 3 are incorrect
    C. More than one of the statements is correct
    D. Only one of the statements is correct

20. The statement below which is MOST inaccurate is:
    A. The supervisor's most important tool in learning whether or not he is communicating well is feedback
    B. Follow-up is essential if useful feedback is to be obtained
    C. Subordinates are entitled, as a matter of right, to explanations from management concerning the reasons for orders or directives
    D. A skilled supervisor is often able to use the grapevine to good advantage

20.____

21. *Since concurrence by those affected is not sought, this kind of communication can be issued with relative ease.* The kind of communication being referred to in this quotation is
    A. autocratic B. democratic C. directive   D. free-rein

21.____

22. The statement below which is LEAST correct is:
    A. Clarity is more important in oral communicating than in written since the readers of a written communication can read it over again
    B. Excessive use of abbreviations in written communications should be avoided
    C. Short sentences with simple words are preferred over complex sentences and difficult words in a written communication
    D. The *newspaper* style of writing ordinarily simplifies expression and facilitates understanding

22.____

23. Which one of the following is the MOST important factor for the department to consider in building a good public image?
    A. A good working relationship with the news media
    B. An efficient community relations program
    C. An efficient system for handling citizen complaints
    D. The proper maintenance of facilities and equipment
    E. The behavior of individuals in their contacts with the public

23.____

24. It has been said that the ability to communicate clearly and concisely is the MOST important single skill of the supervisor.
Consider the following statements:
    I. The adage, *Actions speak louder than words*, has NO application in superior/subordinate communications since good communications are accomplished with words
   II. The environment in which a communication takes place will *rarely* determine its effect
  III. Words are symbolic representations which must be associated with past experience or else they are meaningless

24.____

The choice below which MOST accurately describes the above statements is:
    A. I, II and III are correct
    B. I and II are correct, but III is not

C. I and III are correct, but II is not
D. III is correct, but I and II are not
E. I, II, and III are incorrect

25. According to expert opinion, the effectiveness of an organization is very dependent upon good upward, downward, and lateral communications. Lateral communications are most important to the activity of coordinating the efforts of organizational units. Before real communication can take place at any level, barriers to communication must be recognized, understood, and removed.
Consider the following three statements:
  I. The *principal* barrier to good communications is a failure to establish empathy between sender and receiver
 II. The difference in status or rank between the sender and receiver of a communication may be a communications barrier
III. Communications are easier if they travel upward from subordinate to superior

The choice below which MOST accurately describes the above statements is:
  A. I, II and III are incorrect
  B. I and II are incorrect
  C. I, II, and III are correct
  D. I and II are correct
  E. I and III are incorrect

25. _

KEY (CORRECT ANSWERS)

1. B		11. C	
2. D		12. A	
3. A		13. C	
4. A		14. C	
5. D		15. C	
6. D		16. C	
7. A		17. D	
8. D		18. A	
9. A		19. D	
10. A		20. C	

21. A
22. A
23. E
24. D
25. E

EXAMINATION SECTION
TEST 1

DIRECTIONS: Each question or incomplete statement is followed by several suggested
answers or completions. Select the one that BEST answers the question or
completes the statement. *PRINT THE LETTER OF THE CORRECT ANSWER
IN THE SPACE AT THE RIGHT.*

1.   In public agencies, communications should be based PRIMARILY on a   1._____

   A.   two-way flow from the top down and from the bottom up, most of which should be
given in writing to avoid ambiguity
   B.   multidirection flow among all levels and with outside persons
   C.   rapid, internal one-way flow from the top down
   D.   two-way flow of information, most of which should be given orally for purposes of
clarity

2.   In some organizations, changes in policy or procedures are often communicated by word   2._____
of mouth from supervisors to employees with no prior discussion or exchange of viewpoints with employees.
   This procedure often produces employee dissatisfaction CHIEFLY because

   A.   information is mostly unusable since a considerable amount of time is required to
transmit information
   B.   lower-level supervisors tend to be excessively concerned with minor details
   C.   management has failed to seek employees' advice before making changes
   D.   valuable staff time is lost between decision-making and the implementation of deci-
sions

3.   For good letter writing, you should try to visualize the person to whom you are writing,   3._____
especially if you know him.
   Of the following rules, it is LEAST helpful in such visualization to think of

   A.   the person's likes and dislikes, his concerns, and his needs
   B.   what you would be likely to say if speaking in person
   C.   what you would expect to be asked if speaking in person
   D.   your official position in order to be certain that your words are proper

4.   One approach to good informal letter writing is to make letters sound conversational.   4._____
All of the following practices will usually help to do this EXCEPT:

   A.   If possible, use a style which is similar to the style used when speaking
   B.   Substitute phrases for single words (e.g., *at the present time* for *now)*
   C.   Use contractions of words (e.g., *you're* for *you are)*
   D.   Use ordinary vocabulary when possible

5.   All of the following rules will aid in producing clarity in report-writing EXCEPT: 5._____

   A.   Give specific details or examples, if possible
   B.   Keep related words close together in each sentence
   C.   Present information in sequential order
   D.   Put several thoughts or ideas in each paragraph

6. The one of the following statements about public relations which is MOST accurate is that   6.

    A. in the long run, appearance gains better results than performance
    B. objectivity is decreased if outside public relations consultants are employed
    C. public relations is the responsibility of every employee
    D. public relations should be based on a formal publicity program

7. The form of communication which is usually considered to be MOST personally directed to the intended recipient is the   7.

    A. brochure   B. film   C. letter   D. radio

8. In general, a document that presents an organization's views or opinions on a particular topic is MOST accurately known as a   8.

    A. tear sheet   B. position paper
    C. flyer   D. journal

9. Assume that you have been asked to speak before an organization of persons who oppose a newly announced program in which you are involved. You feel tense about talking to this group.
Which of the following rules generally would be MOST useful in gaining rapport when speaking before the audience?   9.

    A. Impress them with your experience
    B. Stress all areas of disagreement
    C. Talk to the group as to one person
    D. Use formal grammar and language

10. An organization must have an effective public relations program since, at its best, public relations is a bridge to change.
All of the following statements about communication and human behavior have validity EXCEPT: 10.

    A. People are more likely to talk about controversial matters with like-minded people than with those holding other views
    B. The earlier an experience, the more powerful its effect since it influences how later experiences will be interpreted
    C. In periods of social tension, official sources gain increased believability
    D. Those who are already interested in a topic are the ones who are most open to receive new communications about it

11. An employee should be encouraged to talk easily and frankly when he is dealing with his supervisor.
In order to encourage such free communication, it would be MOST appropriate for a supervisor to behave in a(n)   11.

    A. sincere manner; assure the employee that you will deal with him honestly and openly
    B. official manner; you are a supervisor and must always act formally with subordinates

C. investigative manner; you must probe and question to get to a basis of trust
D. unemotional manner; the employee's emotions and background should play no part in your dealings with him

12. Research findings show that an increase in free communication within an agency GEN-ERALLY results in which one of the following?   12.____

    A. Improved morale and productivity
    B. Increased promotional opportunities
    C. An increase in authority
    D. A spirit of honesty

13. Assume that you are a supervisor and your superiors have given you a new-type proce-dure to be followed.   13.____
Before passing this information on to your subordinates, the one of the following actions that you should take FIRST is to

    A. ask your superiors to send out a memorandum to the entire staff
    B. clarify the procedure in your own mind
    C. set up a training course to provide instruction on the new procedure
    D. write a memorandum to your subordinates

14. Communication is necessary for an organization to be effective.   14.____
The one of the following which is LEAST important for most communication systems is that

    A. messages are sent quickly and directly to the person who needs them to operate
    B. information should be conveyed understandably and accurately
    C. the method used to transmit information should be kept secret so that security can be maintained
    D. senders of messages must know how their messages are received and acted upon

15. Which one of the following is the CHIEF advantage of listening willingly to subordinates and encouraging them to talk freely and honestly?   15.____
It

    A. reveals to supervisors the degree to which ideas that are passed down are accepted by subordinates
    B. reduces the participation of subordinates in the operation of the department
    C. encourages subordinates to try for promotion
    D. enables supervisors to learn more readily what the *grapevine* is saying

16. A supervisor may be informed through either oral or written reports.   16.____
Which one of the following is an ADVANTAGE of using oral reports?

    A. There is no need for a formal record of the report.
    B. An exact duplicate of the report is not easily transmitted to others.
    C. A good oral report requires little time for preparation.
    D. An oral report involves two-way communication between a subordinate and his supervisor.

17. Of the following, the MOST important reason why supervisors should communicate effectively with the public is to

    A. improve the public's understanding of information that is important for them to know
    B. establish a friendly relationship
    C. obtain information about the kinds of people who come to the agency
    D. convince the public that services are adequate

17.___

18. Supervisors should generally NOT use phrases like *too hard*, *too easy*, and *a lot* PRINCI- PALLY because such phrases

    A. may be offensive to some minority groups
    B. are too informal
    C. mean different things to different people
    D. are difficult to remember

18.___

19. The ability to communicate clearly and concisely is an important element in effective leadership.
Which of the following statements about oral and written communication is GENER- ALLY true?

    A. Oral communication is more time-consuming.
    B. Written communication is more likely to be misinterpreted.
    C. Oral communication is useful only in emergencies.
    D. Written communication is useful mainly when giving information to fewer than twenty people.

19.___

20. Rumors can often have harmful and disruptive effects on an organization.
Which one of the following is the BEST way to prevent rumors from becoming a prob- lem?

    A. Refuse to act on rumors, thereby making them less believable.
    B. Increase the amount of information passed along by the *grapevine*.
    C. Distribute as much factual information as possible.
    D. Provide training in report writing.

20.___

21. Suppose that a subordinate asks you about a rumor he has heard. The rumor deals with a subject which your superiors consider *confidential*.
Which of the following BEST describes how you should answer the subordinate?
Tell

    A. the subordinate that you don't make the rules and that he should speak to higher ranking officials
    B. the subordinate that you will ask your superior for information
    C. him only that you cannot comment on the matter
    D. him the rumor is not true

21.___

22. Supervisors often find it difficult to *get their message across* when instructing newly appointed employees in their various duties.
The MAIN reason for this is generally that the

22.___

A. duties of the employees have increased
B. supervisor is often so expert in his area that he fails to see it from the learner's point of view
C. supervisor adapts his instruction to the slowest learner in the group
D. new employees are younger, less concerned with job security and more interested in fringe benefits

23. Assume that you are discussing a job problem with an employee under your supervision. During the discussion, you see that the man's eyes are turning away from you and that he is not paying attention.
In order to get the man's attention, you should FIRST

A. ask him to look you in the eye
B. talk to him about sports
C. tell him he is being very rude
D. change your tone of voice

23._____

24. As a supervisor, you may find it necessary to conduct meetings with your subordinates. Of the following, which would be MOST helpful in assuring that a meeting accomplishes the purpose for which it was called?

A. Give notice of the conclusions you would like to reach at the start of the meeting.
B. Delay the start of the meeting until everyone is present.
C. Write down points to be discussed in proper sequence.
D. Make sure everyone is clear on whatever conclusions have been reached and on what must be done after the meeting.

24._____

25. Every supervisor will occasionally be called upon to deliver a reprimand to a subordinate. If done properly, this can greatly help an employee improve his performance.
Which one of the following is NOT a good practice to follow when giving a reprimand?

A. Maintain your composure and temper.
B. Reprimand a subordinate in the presence of other employees so they can learn the same lesson.
C. Try to understand why the employee was not able to perform satisfactorily.
D. Let your knowledge of the man involved determine the exact nature of the reprimand.

25._____

KEY (CORRECT ANSWERS)

1.	C		11.	A
2.	B		12.	A
3.	D		13.	B
4.	B		14.	C
5.	D		15.	A
6.	C		16.	D
7.	C		17.	A
8.	B		18.	C
9.	C		19.	B
10.	C		20.	C

21.	B
22.	B
23.	D
24.	D
25.	B

———

TEST 2

DIRECTIONS: Each question or incomplete statement is followed by several suggested answers or completions. Select the one that BEST answers the question or completes the statement. *PRINT THE LETTER OF THE CORRECT ANSWER IN THE SPACE AT THE RIGHT.*

1. Usually one thinks of communication as a single step, essentially that of transmitting an idea.
   Actually, however, this is only part of a total process, the FIRST step of which should be

   A. the prompt dissemination of the idea to those who may be affected by it
   B. motivating those affected to take the required action
   C. clarifying the idea in one's own mind
   D. deciding to whom the idea is to be communicated

   1.____

2. Research studies on patterns of informal communication have concluded that most indi-viduals in a group tend to be passive recipients of news, while a few make it their busi-ness to spread it around in an organization.
   With this conclusion in mind, it would be MOST correct for the supervisor to attempt to identify these few individuals and

   A. give them the complete facts on important matters in advance of others
   B. inform the other subordinates of the identify of these few individuals so that their influence may be minimized
   C. keep them straight on the facts on important matters
   D. warn them to cease passing along any information to others

   2.____

3. The one of the following which is the PRINCIPAL advantage of making an oral report is that it

   A. affords an immediate opportunity for two-way communication between the subordi-nate and superior
   B. is an easy method for the superior to use in transmitting information to others of equal rank
   C. saves the time of all concerned
   D. permits more precise pinpointing of praise or blame by means of follow-up ques-tions by the superior

   3.____

4. An agency may sometimes undertake a public relations program of a defensive nature.
   With reference to the use of defensive public relations, it would be MOST correct to state that it

   A. is bound to be ineffective since defensive statements, even though supported by factual data, can never hope to even partly overcome the effects of prior unfavor-able attacks
   B. proves that the agency has failed to establish good relationships with newspapers, radio stations, or other means of publicity
   C. shows that the upper echelons of the agency have failed to develop sound public relations procedures and techniques
   D. is sometimes required to aid morale by protecting the agency from unjustified criti-cism and misunderstanding of policies or procedures

   4.____

5. Of the following factors which contribute to possible undesirable public attitudes towards an agency, the one which is MOST susceptible to being changed by the efforts of the individual employee in an organization is that

    A. enforcement of unpopular regulations has offended many individuals
    B. the organization itself has an unsatisfactory reputation
    C. the public is not interested in agency matters
    D. there are many errors in judgment committed by individual subordinates

6. It is not enough for an agency's services to be of a high quality; attention must also be given to the acceptability of these services to the general public.
This statement is GENERALLY

    A. *false;* a superior quality of service automatically wins public support
    B. *true;* the agency cannot generally progress beyond the understanding and support of the public
    C. *false;* the acceptance by the public of agency services determines their quality
    D. *true;* the agency is generally unable to engage in any effective enforcement activity without public support

7. Sustained agency participation in a program sponsored by a community organization is MOST justified when

    A. the achievement of agency objectives in some area depends partly on the activity of this organization
    B. the community organization is attempting to widen the base of participation in all community affairs
    C. the agency is uncertain as to what the community wants
    D. there is an obvious lack of good leadership in a newly formed community organization

8. Of the following, the LEAST likely way in which a records system may serve a supervisor is in

    A. developing a sympathetic and cooperative public attitude toward the agency
    B. improving the quality of supervision by permitting a check on the accomplishment of subordinates
    C. permit a precise prediction of the exact incidences in specific categories for the following year
    D. helping to take the guesswork out of the distribution of the agency

9. Assuming that the *grapevine* in any organization is virtually indestructible, the one of the following which it is MOST important for management to understand is:

    A. What is being spread by means of the *grapevine* and the reason for spreading it
    B. What is being spread by means of the *grapevine* and how it is being spread
    C. Who is involved in spreading the information that is on the *grapevine*
    D. Why those who are involved in spreading the information are doing so

10. When the supervisor writes a report concerning an investigation to which he has been   10.____
assigned, it should be LEAST intended to provide

    A. a permanent official record of relevant information gathered
    B. a summary of case findings limited to facts which tend to indicate the guilt of a sus-
       pect
    C. a statement of the facts on which higher authorities may base a corrective or disci-
       plinary action
    D. other investigators with information so that they may continue with other phases of
       the investigation

11. In survey work, questionnaires rather than interviews are sometimes used.   11.____
The one of the following which is a DISADVANTAGE of the questionnaire method as
compared with the interview is the

    A. difficulty of accurately interpreting the results
    B. problem of maintaining anonymity of the participant
    C. fact that it is relatively uneconomical
    D. requirement of special training for the distribution of questionnaires

12. In his contacts with the public, an employee should attempt to create a good climate of   12.____
support for his agency. This statement is GENERALLY

    A. *false;* such attempts are clearly beyond the scope of his responsibility
    B. *true;* employees of an agency who come in contact with the public have the oppor-
       tunity to affect public relations
    C. *false;* such activity should be restricted to supervisors trained in public relations
       techniques
    D. *true;* the future expansion of the agency depends to a great extent on continued
       public support of the agency

13. The repeated use by a supervisor of a call for volunteers to get a job done is objection-   13.____
able MAINLY because it

    A. may create a feeling of animosity between the volunteers and the non-volunteers
    B. may indicate that the supervisor is avoiding responsibility for making assignments
       which will be most productive
    C. is an indication that the supervisor is not familiar with the individual capabilities of
       his men
    D. is unfair to men who, for valid reasons, do not, or cannot volunteer

14. Of the following statements concerning subordinates' expressions to a supervisor of their   14.____
opinions and feelings concerning work situations, the one which is MOST correct is that

    A. by listening and responding to such expressions the supervisor encourages the
       development of complaints
    B. the lack of such expressions should indicate to the supervisor that there is a high
       level of job satisfaction
    C. the more the supervisor listens to and responds to such expressions, the more he
       demonstrates lack of supervisory ability
    D. by listening and responding to such expressions, the supervisor will enable many
       subordinates to understand and solve their own problems on the job

15. In attempting to motivate employees, rewards are considered preferable to punishment   15.
PRIMARILY because

    A. punishment seldom has any effect on human behavior
    B. punishment usually results in decreased production
    C. supervisors find it difficult to punish
    D. rewards are more likely to result in willing cooperation

16. In an attempt to combat the low morale in his organization, a high-level supervisor publi-   16.
cized an *open-door* policy to allow employees who wished to do so to come to him with
their complaints.
Which of the following is LEAST likely to account for the fact that no employee came in
with a complaint?

    A. Employees are generally reluctant to go over the heads of their immediate supervi-
       sors.
    B. The employees did not feel that management would help them.
    C. The low morale was not due to complaints associated with the job.
    D. The employees felt that they had more to lose than to gain.

17. It is MOST desirable to use written instructions rather than oral instructions for a particu-   17.
lar job when

    A. a mistake on the job will not be serious
    B. the job can be completed in a short time
    C. there is no need to explain the job minutely
    D. the job involves many details

18. If you receive a telephone call regarding a matter which your office does not handle, you   18.
should FIRST

    A. give the caller the telephone number of the proper office so that he can dial again
    B. offer to transfer the caller to the proper office
    C. suggest that the caller re-dial since he probably dialed incorrectly
    D. tell the caller he has reached the wrong office and then hang up

19. When you answer the telephone, the MOST important reason for identifying yourself and   19.
your organization is to

    A. give the caller time to collect his or her thoughts
    B. impress the caller with your courtesy
    C. inform the caller that he or she has reached the right number
    D. set a business-like tone at the beginning of the conversation

20. As soon as you pick up the phone, a very angry caller begins immediately to complain   20.
about city agencies and *red tape*. He says that he has been shifted to two or three different offices. It turns out that he is seeking information which is not immediately available
to you. You believe you know, however, where it can be found. Which of the following
actions is the BEST one for you to take?

    A. To eliminate all confusion, suggest that the caller write the agency stating explicitly
       what he wants.
    B. Apologize by telling the caller how busy city agencies now are, but also tell him
       directly that you do not have the information he needs.

C. Ask for the caller's telephone number and assure him you will call back after you have checked further.

D. Give the caller the name and telephone number of the person who might be able to help, but explain that you are not positive he will get results.

21. Which of the following approaches usually provides the BEST communication in the objectives and values of a new program which is to be introduced?   21._____

    A. A general written description of the program by the program manager for review by those who share responsibility

    B. An effective verbal presentation by the program manager to those affected

    C. Development of the plan and operational approach in carrying out the program by the program manager assisted by his key subordinates

    D. Development of the plan by the program manager's supervisor

22. What is the BEST approach for introducing change?   22._____
A

    A. combination of written and also verbal communication to all personnel affected by the change

    B. general bulletin to all personnel

    C. meeting pointing out all the values of the new approach

    D. written directive to key personnel

23. Of the following, committees are BEST used for   23._____

    A. advising the head of the organization

    B. improving functional work

    C. making executive decisions

    D. making specific planning decisions

24. An effective discussion leader is one who   24._____

    A. announces the problem and his preconceived solution at the start of the discussion

    B. guides and directs the discussion according to pre-arranged outline

    C. interrupts or corrects confused participants to save time

    D. permits anyone to say anything at anytime

25. The human relations movement in management theory is basically concerned with   25._____

    A. counteracting employee unrest

    B. eliminating the *time and motion* man

    C. interrelationships among individuals in organizations

    D. the psychology of the worker

KEY (CORRECT ANSWERS)

1.	C	11.	A
2.	C	12.	B
3.	A	13.	B
4.	D	14.	D
5.	D	15.	D
6.	B	16.	C
7.	A	17.	D
8.	C	18.	B
9.	A	19.	C
10.	B	20.	C

21.	C
22.	A
23.	A
24.	B
25.	C

EXAMINATION SECTION

DIRECTIONS: Each question or incomplete statement is followed by several suggested answers or completions. Select the one that BEST answers the question or completes the statement. *PRINT THE LETTER OF THE CORRECT ANSWER IN THE SPACE AT THE RIGHT.*

Questions 1-5.

DIRECTIONS: Each of Questions 1 through 5 consists of a passage which contains one word that is incorrectly used because it is not in keeping with the meaning that the quotation is evidently intended to convey. Determine which word is incorrectly used. Select from the choices lettered A, B, C, and D the word which, when substituted for the incorrectly used word, would BEST help to convey the meaning of the quotation.

1. Whatever the method, the necessity to keep up with the dynamics of an organization is   1.____
   the point on which many classification plans go awry. The budgetary approach to "positions," for example, often leads to using for recruitment and pay purposes a position
   authorized many years earlier for quite a different purpose than currently contemplated –
   making perhaps the title, the class, and the qualifications required inappropriate to the
   current need. This happens because executives overlook the stability that takes place in
   job duties and fail to reread an initial description of the job before saying, as they scan a
   list of titles, "We should fill this position right away." Once a classification plan is adopted,
   it is pointless to do anything less than provide for continuous, painstaking maintenance
   on a current basis, else once different positions that have actually become similar to
   each other remain in different classes, and some former cognates that have become
   quite different continue in the same class. Such a program often seems expensive. But to
   stint too much on this out-of-pocket cost may create still higher hidden costs growing out
   of lowered morale, poor production, delayed operating programs, excessive pay for simple work, and low pay for responsible work (resulting in poorly qualified executives and
   professional men) – all normal concomitants of inadequate, hasty, or out-of-date classification.

   A. evolution   B. personnel
   C. disapproved   D. forward

2. At first sight, it may seem that there is little or no difference between the usableness of a   2.____
   manual and the degree of its use. But there is a difference. A manual may have all the
   qualities which make up the usable manual and still not be used. Take this instance as an
   example: Suppose you have a satisfactory manual but issue instructions from day to day
   through the avenue of bulletins, memorandums, and other informational releases. Which
   will the employee use, the manual or the bulletin which passes over his desk? He will, of
   course, use the latter, for some obsolete material will not be contained in this manual.
   Here we have a theoretically usable manual which is unused because of the other ave-
   nues by which procedural information may be issued.

   A. countermand   B. discard
   C. intentional   D. worthwhile

3. By reconcentrating control over its operations in a central headquarters, a firm is able to   3._
extend the influence of automation to many, if not all, of its functions – from inventory and
payroll to production, sales, and personnel. In so doing, businesses freeze all the elements of the corporate function in their relationship to one another and to the overall
objectives of the firm. From this total systems concept, companies learn that computers
can accomplish much more than clerical and accounting jobs. Their capabilities can be
tapped to perform the traditional applications (payroll processing, inventory control,
accounts payable, and accounts receivable) as well as newer applications such as spotting deviations from planned programs (exception reporting), adjusting planning schedules, forecasting business trends, simulating market conditions, and solving production
problems. Since the office manager is a manager of information and each of these applications revolves around the processing of data, he must take an active role in studying
and improving the system under his care.

    A.   maintaining   B.   inclusion
    C.   limited   D.   visualize

4. In addition to the formal and acceptance theories of the source of authority, although per-   4._
haps more closely related to the latter, is the belief that authority is generated by personal qualifies of technical competence. Under this heading is the individual who has
made, in effect, subordinates of others through sheer force of personality, and the engi-
neer or economist who exerts influence by furnishing answers or sound advice. These
may have no actual organizational authority, yet their advice may be so eagerly sought
and so unerringly followed that it appears to carry the weight of an order.
But, above all, one cannot discount the importance of formal authority with its institu-
tional foundations. Buttressed by the qualities of leadership implicit in the acceptance
theory, formal authority is basic to the managerial job. Once abrogated, it may be dele-
gated or withheld, used or misused, and be effective in capable hands or be ineffective
in inept hands.

    A.   selected   B.   delegation
    C.   limited   D.   possessed

5. Since managerial operations in organizing, staffing, directing, and controlling are   5._
designed to support the accomplishment of enterprise objectives, planning logically pre-
cedes the execution of all other managerial functions. Although all the functions inter-
mesh in practice, planning is unique in that it establishes the objectives necessary for all
group effort. Besides, plans must be made to accomplish these objectives before the
manager knows what kind of organization relationships and personal qualifications are
needed, along which course subordinates are to be directed, and what kind of control is
to be applied. And, of course, each of the other managerial functions must be planned if
they are to be effective.
Planning and control are inseparable – the Siamese twins of management. Unplanned
action cannot be controlled, for control involves keeping activities on course by correct-
ing deviations from plans. Any attempt to control without plans would be meaningless,
since there is no way anyone can tell whether he is going where he wants to go – the
task of control – unless first he knows where he wants to go – the task of planning.
Plans thus preclude the standards of control.

    A.   coordinating   B.   individual
    C.   furnish   D.   follow

Questions 6-7.

DIRECTIONS: Answer Questions 6 and 7 SOLELY on the basis of information given in the following paragraph.

In-basket tests are often used to assess managerial potential. The exercise consists of a
set of papers that would be likely to be found in the in-basket of an administrator or manager
at any given time, and requires the individuals participating in the examination to indicate how
they would dispose of each item found in the in-basket. In order to handle the in-basket effec-
tively, they must successfully manage their time, refer and assign some work to subordinates,
juggle potentially conflicting appointments and meetings, and arrange for follow-up of prob-
lems generated by the items in the in-basket. In other words, the in-basket test is attempting
to evaluate the participants' abilities to organize their work, set priorities, delegate, control,
and make decisions.

6. According to the above paragraph, to succeed in an in-basket test, an administrator must   6.____

    A. be able to read very quickly
    B. have a great deal of technical knowledge
    C. know when to delegate work
    D. arrange a lot of appointments and meetings

7. According to the above paragraph, all of the following abilities are indications of manage-   7.____
   rial potential EXCEPT the ability to

    A. organize and control   B. manage time
    C. write effective reports   D. make appropriate decisions

Questions 8-9.

DIRECTIONS: Answer Questions 8 and 9 SOLELY on the basis of information given in the following paragraph.

One of the biggest mistakes of government executives with substantial supervisory
responsibility is failing to make careful appraisals of performance during employee probation-
ary periods. Many a later headache could have been avoided by prompt and full appraisal
during the early months of an employee's assignment. There is not much more to say about
this except to emphasize the common prevalence of this oversight, and to underscore that for
its consequences, which are many and sad, the offending managers have no one to blame
but themselves.

8. According to the above passage, probationary periods are   8.____

    A. a mistake, and should not be used by supervisors with large responsibilities
    B. not used properly by government executives
    C. used only for those with supervisory responsibility
    D. the consequence of management mistakes

9. The one of the following conclusions that can MOST appropriately be drawn from the   9.
   above passage is that

   A. management's failure to appraise employees during their probationary period is a
      common occurrence
   B. there is not much to say about probationary periods, because they are unimportant
   C. managers should blame employees for failing to use their probationary periods
      properly
   D. probationary periods are a headache to most managers

Questions 10-12.

DIRECTIONS: Answer Questions 10 through 12 SOLELY on the basis of information given in
              the following paragraph.

*The common sense character of the merit system seems so natural to most Americans
that many people wonder why it should ever have been inoperative. After all, the American
economic system, the most phenomenal the world has ever known, is also founded on a rug-
ged selective process which emphasizes the personal qualities of capacity, industriousness,
and productivity. The criteria may not have always been appropriate and competition has not
always been fair, but competition there was, and the responsibilities and the rewards – with
exceptions, of course – have gone to those who could measure up in terms of intelligence,
knowledge, or perseverance. This has been true not only in the economic area, in the money-
making process, but also in achievement in the professions and other walks of life.*

10. According to the above paragraph, economic rewards in the United States have   10.

    A. always been based on appropriate, fair criteria
    B. only recently been based on a competitive system
    C. not gone to people who compete too ruggedly
    D. usually gone to those people with intelligence, knowledge, and perseverance

11. According to the above passage, a merit system is   11.

    A. an unfair criterion on which to base rewards
    B. unnatural to anyone who is not American
    C. based only on common sense
    D. based on the same principles as the American economic system

12. According to the above passage, it is MOST accurate to say that   12.

    A. the United States has always had a civil service merit system
    B. civil service employees are very rugged
    C. the American economic system has always been based on a merit objective
    D. competition is unique to the American way of life

Questions 13-15.

DIRECTIONS: The management study of employee absence due to sickness is an effective tool in planning. Answer Questions 13 through 15 SOLELY on the data given below.

Number of days absent per worker (sickness)	1	2	3	4	5	6	7	8 or Over
Number of workers	76	23	6	3	1	0	1	0

Total Number of Workers: 400
Period Covered: January 1 - December 31

13. The total number of man days lost due to illness was   13.____

    A. 110   B. 137   C. 144   D. 164

14. What percent of the workers had 4 or more days absence due to sickness?   14.____

    A. .25%   B. 2.5%   C. 1.25%   D. 12.5%

15. Of the 400 workers studied, the number who lost no days due to sickness was   15.____

    A. 190   B. 236   C. 290   D. 346

Questions 16-18.

DIRECTIONS: In the graph below, the lines labeled "A" and "B" represent the cumulative progress in the work of two file clerks, each of whom was given 500 consecutively numbered applications to file in the proper cabinets over a five-day work week. Answer Questions 16 through 18 SOLELY upon the data provided in the graph.

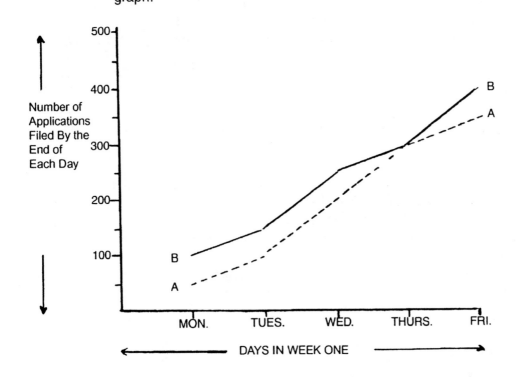

Number of Applications Filed By the End of Each Day

DAYS IN WEEK ONE

16. The day during which the LARGEST number of applications was filed by both clerks was   16._

    A. Monday   B. Tuesday   C. Wednesday   D. Friday

17. At the end of the second day, the percentage of applications STILL to be filed was   17._

    A. 25%   B. 50%   C. 66%   D. 75%

18. Assuming that the production pattern is the same the following week as the week shown   18._
in the chart, the day on which the file clerks will FINISH this assignment will be

    A. Monday   B. Tuesday   C. Wednesday   D. Friday

Questions 19-21.

DIRECTIONS: The following chart shows the differences between the rates of production of employees in Department D in 1996 and 2006. Answer Questions 19 through 21 SOLELY on the basis of the information given in the chart.

Number of Employees Producing Work-Units Within Range in 1996	Number of Work-Units Produced	Number of Employees Producing Work-Units Within Range in 2006
7	500 - 1000	4
14	1001 - 1500	11
26	1501 - 2000	28
22	2001 - 2500	36
17	2501 - 3000	39
10	3001 - 3500	23
4	3501 - 4000	9

19. Assuming that within each range of work-units produced the average production was at   19._
the mid-point at that range (e.g., category 500 - 1000 = 750), then the AVERAGE number
of work-units produced per employee in 1996 fell into the range

    A. 1001 - 1500   B. 1501 - 2000
    C. 2001 - 2500   D. 2501 - 3000

20. The ratio of the number of employees producing more than 2000 work-units in 1996 to   20._
the number of employees producing more than 2000 work-units in 2006 is *most nearly*

    A. 1:2   B. 2:3   C. 3:4   D. 4:5

21. In Department D, which of the following were GREATER in 2006 than in 1996?   21._
      I.   Total number of employees
     II.   Total number of work-units produced
    III.   Number of employees producing 2000 or fewer work-units
The CORRECT answer is:

    A. I, II, III   B. I, II
    C. I, III   D. II, III

22. Unit S's production fluctuated substantially from one year to another. In 2004, Unit S's production was 100% greater than in 2003. In 2005, production decreased by 25% from 2004. In 2006, Unit S's production was 10% greater than in 2005.
On the basis of this information, it is CORRECT to conclude that Unit S's production in 2006 exceeded Unit S's production in 2003 by

   A. 65%   B. 85%   C. 95%   D. 135%

23. Agency "X" is moving into a new building. It has 1500 employees presently on its staff and does not contemplate much variance from this level. The new building contains 100 available offices, each with a maximum capacity of 30 employees. It has been decided that only 2/3 of the maximum capacity of each office will be utilized. The TOTAL number of offices that will be occupied by Agency "X" is

   A. 30   B. 66   C. 75   D. 90

24. One typist completes a form letter every 5 minutes and another typist completes one every 6 minutes.
If the two typists start together, they will again start typing new letters simultaneously _____ minutes later and will have completed ____ letters by that time.

   A. 11; 30   B. 12; 24   C. 24; 12   D. 30; 11

25. During one week, a machine operator produces 10 fewer pages per hour of work than he usually does. If it ordinarily takes him six hours to produce a 300-page report, it will take him____hours LONGER to produce that same 300-page report during the week when he produces MORE slowly.

   A. $1\frac{1}{2}$ B. $1\frac{2}{3}$ C. 2   D. $2\frac{3}{4}$

KEY (CORRECT ANSWERS)

1. A	11. D
2. D	12. C
3. D	13. D
4. D	14. C
5. C	15. C
6. C	16. C
7. C	17. D
8. B	18. B
9. A	19. C
10. D	20. A

21. B
22. A
23. C
24. D
25. A

———

EXAMINATION SECTION
TEST 1

DIRECTIONS: Each question or incomplete statement is followed by several suggested answers or completions. Select the one that BEST answers the question or completes the statement. *PRINT THE LETTER OF THE CORRECT ANSWER IN THE SPACE AT THE RIGHT.*

1. Of the following, an important goal of the reorganization of a human services agency is to

    A. strengthen the centralization of services at agency headquarters
    B. provide services within the neighborhoods according to local needs
    C. equalize the distribution of responsibilities between headquarters and neighborhood offices
    D. give more authority and responsibility to neighborhood offices than to headquarters

    1.____

2. The one of the following which is NOT a purpose of the movement toward decentralization of city government is to

    A. reduce citizen alienation
    B. bolster city services
    C. respond to local needs
    D. discourage the local power structure

    2.____

3. Of the following, the MOST desirable way to strengthen the capacity of communities to contribute to the solution of their own problems is to

    A. encourage participation of local residents in service planning and delivery
    B. establish city-wide job training programs
    C. reduce technical assistance to local small business so that they will learn by experience
    D. make local residents accountable to government agencies for funds and services provided

    3.____

4. In organizing the residents of a disadvantaged neighborhood to develop projects for community improvement, the MOST effective of the following approaches is to

    A. concentrate on the group with most members
    B. devote more attention to groups which have vested interests
    C. try to include all groups
    D. give special consideration to official groups

    4.____

5. The one of the following which has been the MOST common problem which occurs when attempts are made to obtain community participation in a project such as a neighborhood improvement program is

    A. domination by an aggressive but unrepresentative group
    B. public opposition by representatives of government agencies
    C. fragmentation and disruption of community services
    D. serious deterioration in the quality of services

    5.____

6. Of the following, the MOST important aim of the community organizer in his early con-   6.
tacts with a community group should be to

   A. build a core of common interests
   B. establish himself as a forceful leader who can make decisions
   C. inform the group of its legal rights
   D. curb discussion of opposing viewpoints in order to develop harmonious relations

7. The one of the following which is the BEST method of encouraging neighborhood people   7.
to attend a community meeting is to

   A. send out notices at least a week in advance
   B. set up an agenda that deals with issues of serious local concern
   C. invite a prominent public figure to address the meeting
   D. send invitations to community people with similar viewpoints on the problem to be
   discussed

8. A basic difference between pure experimental research and action research is that   8.
experimental research is primarily concerned with the analysis of data for scientific or
technological generalization, while action research is

   A. based on the results of trial and error
   B. designed to effect improvement in an on–going process
   C. intuitive rather than scientific in nature
   D. primarily concerned with the analysis of data for universal generalization

9. Assume that a community worker is assigned to organize a client group to participate in   9.
planning for services they particularly need.
Of the following, it would be LEAST important for the organizer to become familiar with
the

   A. local store owners   B. neighborhood resources
   C. potential leaders   D. informal leaders

10. Of the following, the factor which is MOST important in encouraging a high level of local   10.
participation in community projects is the

   A. degree of sophistication of the local people
   B. attitudes of the community development workers towards the local people
   C. amount of money available for training
   D. amount of time available for stimulation of community interest

11. Assume that you are the discussion leader of a meeting of a group of residents of a pov-   11.
erty area, many of whom are against a proposal to locate a methadone maintenance
treatment center in the neighborhood.
The BEST way for you to assist the group is to help them FIRST to

   A. get to know each other on an informal basis
   B. understand the overall background of the drug problem and the need for such a
   facility in the community
   C. concentrate on all the issues until they iron out conflicting viewpoints
   D. discuss the pros and cons briefly, take a vote, and accept the decision of the major-
   ity

12. Of the following, the MOST important aim of the community development process is pri- 12.____
marily to strengthen the

    A. long–established social and political pattern of relationships
    B. influence of dominant ethnic and religious groups
    C. long–standing power of traditional central government
    D. positive impulses of people working toward a common goal

13. One method of influencing human behavior is based upon an optimistic belief in human 13.____
potential for development and betterment.
Workers in the human services who apply this method expect that it will

    A. awaken initiative in clients
    B. demand a pre–chosen response from clients
    C. give clients a spirit of competition
    D. get clients to accept new ideas

14. The community development process is MOST effective when 14.____

    A. final decisions are made solely by the community development expediters
    B. a firm plan is made after a project gets under way
    C. decisions are left in the hands of community people
    D. militant factions are permitted to take a firm stand

15. Of the following, the MOST significant indication that an organizer of a community group 15.____
has done an effective job would be a situation where the group

    A. continues to grow in size and strength after the organizer has departed
    B. disperses after the organizer has departed because it has fulfilled its purpose
    C. attains its goals only under the organizer's guidance
    D. has a warm and friendly relationship with the organizer

16. The MAIN purpose of group discussion of community issues by local residents is to 16.____

    A. present a predetermined point of view
    B. provide an outlet for release of the participants' aggressions
    C. consider and work through common problems
    D. improve relationships among participants

17. Of the following, the MOST important reason why the community development worker in 17.____
a disadvantaged community of a major metropolis should seek to understand the motiva-
tions of the local residents is that he will be more capable of assisting them in developing

    A. self–help activities
    B. projects which will get publicity
    C. an overall master plan
    D. projects which do not require technical assistance

18. At certain times, there is a tendency for community groups to disregard democratic pro- 18.___
cedures in making decisions, particularly in a situation where

    A. action depends on availability of community services
    B. the executive board makes the decision
    C. there is need for speedy action
    D. there is no sound basis for the decision

19. The employment of residents of poverty areas with little or no educational qualifications 19.___
to assist professional staff members in working with clients of human services agencies
is GENERALLY considered

    A. *advisable,* mainly because local paraprofessionals can be expected to bridge the
gap between the middle class professional worker and lower class recipients of
service
    B. *inadvisable,* mainly because the employment of workers who are not professionals
will lower the professional standards of the agency's staff
    C. *advisable,* mainly because employment of paraprofes–sional local residents will
save agency funds
    D. *inadvisable,* mainly because clients will receive services of poorer quality than ser-
vices provided by professional workers

20. The social work activist who was a leader in the movement to achieve welfare reform by 20.___
organizing welfare clients and encouraging the poor to demand their legal rights to public
assistance is (was)

    A. Saul Alinsky   B. Richard Cloward
    C. Bertram Beck   D. Jesse Gray

Questions 21–26.

DIRECTIONS: Questions 21 through 26 are to be answered SOLELY on the basis of the following passage.

Too often in the past, society has accepted the existing social welfare programs, prefer-
ring to tinker with refinements when fundamental reform was in order. It has been a *demeaning,* degrading welfare system in which the instrument of government was wrongfully and
ineptly used. It has been a system which has only alienated those forced to benefit from it and
demoralized those who had to administer it at the level where the pain was clearly visible.

There is a need to put this nation on a course in which cash benefits, providing a basic
level or support, are conferred in such a way as to intrude as little as possible into privacy and
self–respect. It is difficult to define a basic level of support, no matter how high or low it might
be set. In the end, however, the decision is not determined so much by how much is truly adequate for a family to meet all of its needs, but by the resources available to carry out the prom-
ise. That may be a harsh fact of life but it is also just that—a fact of life.

21. Of the following, the MOST suitable title for the above passage would be

    21.____

    A.   THE NEED FOR GOVERNMENT CONTROL OF WELFARE
    B.   DETERMINING THE BASIC LEVEL OF SUPPORT
    C.   THE NEED FOR. WELFARE REFORM
    D.   THE ELIMINATION OF WELFARE PROGRAMS

22. In this passage, the author's GREATEST criticism of the welfare system is that it is too

    22.____

    A.   disrespectful of recipients
    B.   expensive to administer
    C.   limited by regulations
    D.   widespread in application

23. According to the passage, the basic level of support is ACTUALLY determined by

    23.____

    A.   how much is required for a family to meet all of its needs
    B.   the age of the recipients
    C.   how difficult it is to administer the program
    D.   the economic resources of the nation

24. In this passage, the author does NOT argue for

    24.____

    A.   a work Incentive system   B.   a basic level of support
    C.   cash benefits   D.   the privacy of recipients

25. As used in the above passage, the italicized word *demeaning* means MOST NEARLY

    25.____

    A.   ineffective   B.   expensive
    C.   overburdened   D.   humiliating

26. As used in the above passage, the italicized, word *ineptly* means MOST NEARLY

    26.____

    A.   foolishly   B.   unsuccessfully
    C.   unskillfully   D.   unhappily

Questions 27–30.

DIRECTIONS: Questions 27 through 30 are to be answered SOLELY on the basis of the following paragraph.

    The unemployment rate, which counts those unemployed in the sense that they are actively looking for work and unable to find it, gives a relatively *superficial* index of economic conditions in a community. A better index is the subemployment rate which includes the unemployment rate and also includes those working part–time while they are trying to get full–time work; those heads of households under 65 years of age who earn less than $240 per week working full–time, and those individuals under 65 who are not heads of households and earn less than $220 per week in a full–time job; and an estimate of the males *not counted,* which is a very real concern in ghetto areas.

27. Of the following, the MOST suitable title for the above paragraph would be   27.

    A. EMPLOYMENT IN THE UNITED STATES
    B. PART–TIME WORKERS AND THE ECONOMY
    C. THE LABOR MARKET AND THE COMMUNITY
    D. TWO INDICATORS OF ECONOMIC CONDITIONS

28. On the basis of the paragraph, which of the following statements is CORRECT?   28.
The

    A. unemployment rate includes everyone who is not fully employed
    B. subemployment rate is higher than the unemployment rate
    C. unemployment rate gives a more complex picture of the economic situation than the subemployment rate
    D. subemployment rate indicates how many part–time workers are dissatisfied with the number of hours they work per week

29. As used in the above paragraph, the italicized word *superficial* means MOST NEARLY   29.

    A. exaggerated   B. official
    C. surface   D. current

30. According to the paragraph, which of the following is included in the subemployment   30.
rate?

    A. Everyone who is unemployed
    B. All part–time workers
    C. Everyone under 65 who earns less than $224 per week in a full–time job
    D. All heads of households who earn less than $240 per week in a full–time job

----

KEY (CORRECT ANSWERS)

1.	B	11.	B	21.	C
2.	D	12.	D	22.	A
3.	A	13.	A	23.	D
4.	C	14.	C	24.	A
5.	A	15.	A	25.	D
6.	A	16.	C	26.	C
7.	B	17.	A	27.	D
8.	B	18.	C	28.	B
9.	A	19.	A	29.	C
10.	B	20.	B	30.	C

TEST 2

DIRECTIONS: Each question or incomplete statement is followed by several suggested answers or completions. Select the one that BEST answers the question or completes the statement. *PRINT THE LETTER OF THE CORRECT ANSWER IN THE SPACE AT THE RIGHT.*

1. The one of the following which accounts for the LARGEST portion of the budget of the Human Resources Administration is

   A. personnel and support services
   B. public assistance and medicaid
   C. services to children and youth
   D. community organization and development

   1.____

2. According to the latest statistics published by the U. S. Department of Health, Education and Welfare, the state which spent the LARGEST amount of money per person for public assistance is

   A. California   B. Massachusetts
   C. Pennsylvania   D. New York

   2.____

3. According to the MOST recent U.S. Census Bureau Report, the group living in New York City which has the lowest income level is the

   A. Blacks   B. Puerto Ricans
   C. Dominicans   D. Haitians

   3.____

4. The group that contains the LARGEST number of individuals receiving public assistance is

   A. children under working age
   B. unemployed heads of families
   C. the aged, disabled, and blind
   D. unemployed single persons

   4.____

5. A MAJOR difficulty faced by new arrivals to cities since 1970 which did not exist for earlier European immigrants is the fact that the majority of present–day arrivals

   A. must forfeit their native culture patterns
   B. have an obviously darker skin color than most longtime residents
   C. have little education
   D. have few occupational skills

   5.____

6. Generally speaking, low–income persons do not make maximum use of opportunities and services available to them MAINLY because

   A. most paraprofessional workers, while sincere in the desire to serve, are unable to reach the hard core
   B. much of the routine paperwork in public assistance programs is now assigned to paraprofessional workers
   C. they have become increasingly self–reliant and prefer to cope with their problems without help
   D. they lack the confidence and know–how necessary to make their needs known to the proper persons or agencies

   6.____

7. The one of the following problems which has once again become a serious concern of   7.
youth services agencies is the

    A. increasing high school drop–out rate
    B. resurgence of fighting youth gangs
    C. spread of youth narcotics addiction
    D. lack of recreation programs

8. Of the following, the MOST recent development with regard to welfare recipients is   8.

    A. introduction of the declaration of need instead of an investigation of eligibility
    B. a major emphasis on employment programs
    C. increased use of casework therapy and psychiatric counseling
    D. acceptance of narcotics addicts for home relief

9. According to a recent decision by a federal court, regular reporting at state employment   9.
service offices to pick up checks or accept work can NO LONGER be required of recipients of

    A. Aid to the Disabled
    B. Home Relief
    C. Aid to Dependent Children
    D. Medicaid

10. A BASIC objective of the proposal for revenue sharing under consideration by the U.S.   10.
Congress is to provide

    A. state and local governments with new sources of revenue from the federal govern-
ment and greater control over how this revenue is spent
    B. the federal government with greater control over spending of certain federally–
raised tax revenues
    C. safeguards against improper allocation of funds by state and local officials and
incentives to states for reporting violations by local government
    D. a method of sharing federal revenue with the states and localities in accordance
with their required expenditures for public assistance and social welfare services

11. The component of the human services agency which sets policy for the administration,   11.
coordination, and allocation of funds for community action programs is the

    A. Community Development Agency
    B. Department of Social Services
    C. Council on Poverty
    D. Manpower and Career Development Agency

12. The policies of the Council Against Poverty are carried out by the   12.

    A. Community Development Agency
    B. Manpower and Career Development Agency
    C. Department of Social Services
    D. Neighborhood Manpower Service Centers

13. The reorganization of the human services agency has established the unit of organization for provisions of services at the neighborhood level as the

    A. designated poverty area
    B. human resources district
    C. catchment area
    D. census tract

    13.____

14. The Child Development Commission established by the Agency for Child Development can BEST be described as a group comprised of

    A. professionals in child psychology and early childhood education who will consult with Agency staff members on policy and programs
    B. parents, community organizations, and concerned citizens who will help the Agency determine, review, and modify policies and guidelines for childcare services
    C. child–care experts who will provide technical assistance to private groups that want to develop early childhood centers
    D. professionals who will offer health and nutrition consultation and a variety of support and referral services for children and parents

    14.____

15. The BASIC purpose of the office of Community Social Services in the Department of Social Services is to

    A. help local community leaders establish liaison with private social service agencies in their communities
    B. determine the social service needs of each community and provide services in accordance with these needs
    C. provide information and referral to all HRA services existing in a particular community and to services provided by other city agencies and private organizations
    D. assume responsibility for a variety of social services mandated by federal and state regulations

    15.____

16. The Social Service Exchange is CORRECTLY described as a

    A. recruitment center for the training and placement of volunteers for social and health agencies
    B. center which maintains a central index of case records of families and individuals known to social and health agencies
    C. center which provides information about and makes referrals to social and health agencies and proprietary nursing homes
    D. confidential advisory service to help potential contributors evaluate local voluntary health and welfare agencies

    16.____

17. Which one of the following is an IMPORTANT purpose of the formation of the Office of Special Services for Children in the Department of Social Services?

    A. Greater programmatic integration of the protective and supportive services to children who are abused, neglected, dependent, delinquent, or in need of services
    B. More professional attention to child abuse cases and prompt court action to penalize parents of abused or neglected children
    C. Separation of programs and facilities for children adjudged to be delinquent from special services for other dependent, abused, or neglected children
    D. Increased attention to home–finding and foster care and adoption services rather than institutional care for dependent children

    17.____

18. The one of the following which is provided by the Department of Social Services for current, former, and potential public assistance recipients ONLY is _____ services.

    A. information   B. child welfare
    C. referral   D. homemaker

18.___

19. A MAJOR goal of the Department of Social Services which is part of the reorganization and the separation of income maintenance from social services is to

    A. limit the provision of public social services to those persons who are eligible for public assistance
    B. make public social services available to all persons, whether or not they require financial assistance
    C. refer clients who require social services to private agencies wherever possible
    D. emphasize casework treatment and referral of clients for psychiatric services rather than programs to effect environmental change

19.___

20. Of the following, the MAIN functions of the Manpower and Career Development Agency (MCDA) of a human services agency are to

    A. train the unskilled, upgrade existing skills, develop job opportunities, and place newly–trained people in jobs
    B. operate manpower, recruitment, and testing centers under contract with private organizations
    C. provide remedial education and follow–up for dis–advantaged potential college students and vocational testing and counseling for veterans and ex–addicts
    D. provide job development, interviewing and placement, and manpower research services

20.___

Questions 21–25.

DIRECTIONS: Questions 21 through 25 are to be answered SOLELY on the diagram presented below.

HOW THE INNER–CITY FAMILY IN URBANVILLE SPENDS ITS MONEY

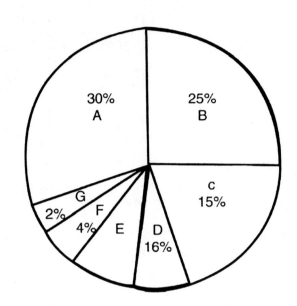

A. Food
B. Shelter
C. Clothing
D. Household Operation
E. Medical Care
F. Transportation
G. Miscellaneous

21. According to the above diagram, the percentage spent on medical care is   21._____

    A. 7%   B. 8%   C. 16%   D. 18%

22. According to the above diagram, the total percentage spent on food, shelter, and clothing   22._____
    is

    A. 55%   B. 60%   C. 70%   D. 75%

23. In a typical period, if the family spent $60 on transportation, how much did it spend on   23._____
    household operation?

    A. $240   B. $384   C. $600   D. $960

24. If the family income is $250 a week, how much does it spend on transportation each   24._____
    year?

    A. $120   B. $520   C. $1,200   D. $5,200

25. Assume that the annual income of a family was $10,800 for several years. Last year, the   25._____
    income went up 5%, and the family then tripled the typical percentage for household
    operation.
    The amount spent on this item last year was MOST NEARLY

    A. $1,782   B. $2,268   C. $2,592   D. $5,442

Questions 26–30.

DIRECTIONS: Questions 26 through 30 are to be answered SOLELY on the basis of the table
              presented below.

AFDC FAMILY MEMBERS IN URBANVILLE
Referred to and Enrolled in WIN Program, 2001-2002

	Referred		Enrolled	
Family Member	2001	2002	2001	2002
Mother	1,091	1,306	730	877
Father	743	950	520	731
Child, age 16 and over	170	222	150	184

26. According to the above table, how many AFDC family members were referred to WIN in 2002?

    A. 1,792   B. 2,004   C. 2,388   D. 2,478

27. According to the above table, the number of AFDC children 16 and over who were enrolled in WIN in 2002 was GREATER than the number enrolled in 2001 by

    A. 12   B. 34   C. 38   D. 52

28. According to the above table, the number of AFDC mothers who were enrolled in 2002 INCREASED over the number enrolled in 2001 MOST NEARLY by

    A. 20%   B. 32%   C. 54%   D. 83%

29. In 2003, if the number of AFDC mothers referred to WIN increases 5% over 2002, the number of fathers referred increases 8% over 2002, and the number of children referred increases 5% over 2002, the TOTAL number of AFDC family members that will be referred in 2003 is MOST NEARLY

    A. 1,424   B. 1,524   C. 3,130   D. 3,990

30. According to the above table, the percentage of AFDC fathers NOT enrolled in WIN in 2002 of the number referred that year is MOST NEARLY

    A. 23%   B. 25%   C. 71%   D. 77%

KEY (CORRECT ANSWERS)

1.	B	11.	B	21.	B
2.	D	12.	D	22.	C
3.	D	13.	B	23.	A
4.	A	14.	B	24.	B
5.	B	15.	B	25.	D
6.	D	16.	C	26.	D
7.	B	17.	B	27.	B
8.	B	18.	A	28.	A
9.	C	19.	A	29.	C
10.	A	20.	D	30.	A

READING COMPREHENSION
UNDERSTANDING AND INTERPRETING WRITTEN MATERIAL
TEST 1

DIRECTIONS: Each question or incomplete statement is followed by several suggested answers or completions. Select the one that BEST answers the question or completes the statement. *PRINT THE LETTER OF THE CORRECT ANSWER IN THE SPACE AT THE RIGHT.*

DIRECTIONS FOR THIS SECTION:
   All questions are to be answered SOLELY on the basis of the information contained in the passage.

Questions 1-3.

   It is common knowledge that ability to do a particular job and performance on the job do not always go hand in hand.   Persons with great potential abilities sometimes fall down on the job because of laziness or lack of interest in the job, while persons with mediocre talents have often achieved excellent results through their industry and their loyalty to the interests of their employers.   It is clear, therefore, that in a balanced personnel program, measures of employee ability need to be supplemented by measures of employee performance, for the final test of any employee is his performance on the job.

1.   The *MOST* accurate of the following statements, on the basis of the above paragraph, is that
   A.   employees who lack ability are usually not industrious
   B.   an employee's attitudes are more important than his abilities
   C.   mediocre employees who are interested in their work are preferable to employees who possess great ability
   D.   superior capacity for performance should be supplemented with proper attitudes

1._____

2.   On the basis of the above paragraph, the employee of most value to his employer is *NOT* necessarily the one who
   A.   best understands the significance of his duties
   B.   achieves excellent results
   C.   possesses the greatest talents
   D.   produces the greatest amount of work

2._____

3.   According to the above paragraph, an employee's efficiency is *BEST* determined by an
   A.   appraisal of his interest in his work
   B.   evaluation of the work performed by him
   C.   appraisal of his loyalty to his employer
   D.   evaluation of his potential ability to perform his work

3._____

Questions 4-5.

The cabinet shall be *fabricated* entirely of 22-gage stainless steel with #4 satin finish on all exposed surfaces.   The face trim shall be one-piece construction with no mitres or welding, 1" wide and 1/4" to the wall.   All doors shall be mounted on heavy-duty stainless steel piano hinges and have a concealed lock.

4.   As used in the above paragraph, the word *fabricated* means, most nearly,   4.___
           A.   made   B.   designed   C.   cut   D.   plated

5.   According to the above paragraph, a satin finish is to be used on surfaces   5.___
           A.   to be welded   B.   that are visible
           C.   on which the hinges are mounted
           D.   that are to be covered

Questions 6-10.

Many people still think accidents just happen – that they are due to bad luck. Nothing could be further from the truth.

Evidence of this is in the drop in accidents among employees of the City since the Safety Program started.

The one-out-of-a-hundred accidents that cannot be prevented might be called "Acts of God." They are things like lightning, earthquakes, tornadoes, and tidal waves that we are powerless to prevent – although we can take precautions against them which will cut down the accident rate.

The other ninety-nine percent of the accidents clearly have a man-made cause. If you trace back far enough, you'll find that some where, somehow, someone could have done something to prevent these accidents.   For just about every accident, there is some fellow who fouled up.   He didn't protect himself, he didn't use the right equipment, he wasn't alert, he lost his temper, he didn't have his mind on his work, he was "kidding around," or he took a shortcut because he was just too lazy.

We must all work together to improve safety and prevent injury and death.

6.   The *one* of the following titles which *BEST* describes the subject matter of   6.__
           the above passage is:
           A.   Acts of God
           B.   The Importance of Safety Consciousness
           C.   Safety in the City   D.   Working Together

7.   After the City began to operate a safety program, it was found that   7.__
           A.   the number of accidents was reduced
           B.   production decreased
           C.   accidents stayed the same but employees were more careful
           D.   the element of bad luck did not change

8.   *One* cause of accidents that is *NOT* mentioned in the above passage is   8.__
           A.   failure to keep alert   B.   taking a short cut
           C.   using the wrong equipment   D.   working too fast

9. The number of accidents caused by such things as hurricanes can be
    A. changed only by an "Act of God"
    B. eliminated by strict adherence to safety rules
    C. increased by being too careful
    D. reduced by proper safety precautions

9._____

10. The percentage of accidents that occur as a result of things that cannot be prevented is, approximately,
    A. 1 percent   B. 10 percent   C. 50 percent   D. 99 percent

10._____

Questions 11-15.

The most effective control mechanism to prevent gross incompetence on the part of public employees is a good personnel program. The personnel officer in the line departments and the central personnel agency should exert positive leadership to raise levels of performance. Although the key factor is the quality of the personnel recruited, staff members other than personnel officers can make important contributions to efficiency. Administrative analysts, now employed in many agencies, make detailed studies of organization and procedures, with the purpose of eliminating delays, waste, and other inefficiencies. Efficiency is, however, more than a question of good organization and procedures; it is also the product of the attitudes and values of the public employees. Personal motivation can provide the will to be efficient. The best management studies will not result in substantial improvement of the performance of those employees who feel no great urge to work up to their abilities.

11. The passage indicates that the *key* factor in preventing gross incompetence of public employees is the
    A. hiring of administrative analysts to assist personnel people
    B. utilization of effective management studies
    C. overlapping of responsibility
    D. quality of the employees hired

11._____

12. According to the above passage, the central personnel agency staff should
    A. work more closely with administrative analysts in the line departments than with personnel officers
    B. make a serious effort to avoid jurisdictional conflicts with personnel officers in line departments
    C. contribute to improving the quality of work of public employees
    D. engage in a comprehensive program to change the public's negative image of public employees

12._____

13. The author of the passage believes that efficiency in an organization can *BEST* be brought about by
    A. eliminating ineffective control mechanisms
    B. instituting sound organizational procedures
    C. promoting competent personnel
    D. recruiting people with desire to do good work

13._____

14. According to the passage, the purpose of administrative analysis in a public agency is to   14.__
    - A. *prevent* injustice to the public employee
    - B. *promote* the efficiency of the agency
    - C. *protect* the interests of the public
    - D. *ensure* the observance of procedural due process

15. The passage *implies* that a considerable rise in the quality of work of public employees can be brought about by   15.__
    - A. encouraging positive employee attitudes toward work
    - B. controlling personnel officers who exceed their powers
    - C. creating warm personal associations among public employees in an agency
    - D. closing loopholes in personnel organizations and procedures

Questions 16-25.   Answer questions 16 through 25 based on the following instructions:

INSTRUCTIONS FOR PREPARATION AND PLACEMENT OF RAT BAIT

a. Fresh baits are the most acceptable to rats, so mix only enough bait for curr needs.   Use a binder of molasses or of vegetable, mineral or fish oil in cerea dry baits to hold the poison and the dry bait together and to aid in mixing.

b. Mix an emetic, usually tartar emetic, with zinc phosphide and other more tox bait formulations to protect animals other than rodents, even though acceptability of such baits to the rodents is thereby reduced.

c. Mix bait as directed.   Too much poison may give the bait a strong taste or o Too little will not kill but may result in "bait shyness." Excessive amounts of poison increase the danger to man and to domestic animals.

d. Mix baits well.   Poor mixing results in non-uniform baits and poor kills and speeds development of bait shyness.   Mechanical bait-mixing equipment is necessary where large quantities of bait are mixed routinely.

e. Clearly label poisons and mixing equipment.   Do not use bait-mixing equipment for other purposes.   Lock up poisons and mixing equipment whe not in use.   Treat all poisons with respect. Read and follow all label instructi Avoid inhaling powders or getting poisons on hands, clothes, or utensils from which they may reach the mouth.   Wear rubber gloves when handling pois Always mix poisons in a well-ventilated place, particularly when mixing dry ingredients.

f. If anti-coagulant baits are used, they should be placed in paper, metal, or pla pie plates or in permanent bait stations.   Be liberal in baiting.   For anti-coagulants to be fully effective, repeated doses must be consumed by ev rodent at a given location for a period of five or more consecutive days.

g. Protect animals other than domestic rodents, and shield baits from the weat under shelter or with bait boxes, boards, pipes, or cans.

h. Note locations of all bait containers so that inspections can be made rapidly and the bait that has been consumed can be quickly replaced. (Bait consumption is generally heavy right after initial placement, making daily inspection and replacement advisable for the first 3 days after regular feeding begins.)

i. At each inspection, smooth the surface of the baits so that new signs of feeding will show readily. Replace moldy, wet, caked, or insect-infested baits with fresh ones. If a bait remains undisturbed for several successive inspections, move it to an area showing fresh rodent signs.

j. Use shallow bait containers fastened to the floor, or containers of sufficient weight to prevent the rodents from overturning them or dragging them to their burrows. A roofing tack driven through metal or fiber containers into the floor reduces spillage.

k. When single-dose poisons are used, wrap one-shot poison foot baits in 4" x 4" paper squares to form "torpedoes" about the size of a large olive. These may be tossed readily into otherwise inaccessible places. If several types of bait such as meat, fish, or cereal are to be distributed at the same time, a different color of paper should be used for each of the various types of bait.

l. Be generous with baits. Too few baits, or poorly-placed baits, may miss many rodents. Bait liberally where signs of rat activity are numerous and recent. In light or moderate infestations, torpedoes containing a single-dose poison, such as reds quill, have given good control when applied at a minimum rate of 20 baits per private residence. As many as 100 to 200 baits may be required for premises with heavy rodent infestations .

m. Place baits in hidden sites out of reach of children and pets.

n. Inspect and rebait as needed, using another poison and another bait material when the rats become shy of the original baits.

16. According to the above instructions, if you find, upon inspection, that your baits are overrun with insects, you should   16._____
    A. replace the baits with fresh baits
    B. move the baits to another station
    C. add more rodenticide to the baits and re-mix them
    D. apply the appropriate insecticide to the baits

17. According to the above instructions, if you want to make sure you do *NOT* get poor kills, you should   17._____
    A. mix large quantities of baits routinely
    B. stick to one poison   C. mix the baits well
    D. use deep bait containers that cannot be easily overturned

18. According to the above instructions, the equipment which is used for mixing bait should be   18._____
    A. cleaned routinely   B. mechanically easy to handle
    C. easily disposable   D. labeled clearly

19. According to the above instructions, making the surface of the bait smooth every time that you inspect the bait containers is
    19._
    A. proper because it disturbs the insect infestation of the bait
    B. improper because it will make the bait even less uniform if it was already mixed poorly
    C. proper because it will help you determine if new signs of feeding are present
    D. improper because it increases the presence of human odor on the bait and discourages rodents

20. According to the above instructions, if you are making a bait with zinc phosphide, it is *MOST* important to
    20._
    A. prepare a generous amount so you can bait liberally where signs of rat activity are numerous
    B. use molasses to insure that the bait will be uniform
    C. shield the bait from the weather
    D. mix an emetic with the bait

21. According to the above instructions, you should substitute one poison for another poison when the
    21._
    A. bait consumption is heavy after initial placement
    B. rodents become shy of the original baits
    C. poison is dangerous to domestic animals
    D. rodents are able to drag the baits to their burrows

22. According to the above instructions, when you handle poisons, you should
    22._
    A. use mechanical bait-making equipment
    B. wear rubber gloves
    C. never place them in paper plates
    D. always mix them with moist ingredients

23. According to the above instructions, if you plan to distribute several types of bait at the same time in the form of "torpedoes," you should
    23._
    A. select only anti-coagulant baits for this purpose
    B. reduce the possibility of bait spillage by driving a roofing tack through the container into the floor
    C. use a different color of paper for each of the various types of bait
    D. make sure that the rodent does not consume repeated doses for more than a period of five consecutive days at the same location

24. According to the above instructions, mixing too much poison in the bait
    24._
    A. may bring about bait shyness
    B. permits you to make less frequent re-inspections
    C. increases the danger to other life
    D. may be necessary when anti-coagulants are used

25. According to the above instructions, if grain is to be used as bait,
    25._
    A. rodents will not accept it if it is mixed with fish oil
    B. you will only be able to make "torpedoes"
    C. it will not be necessary to check the bait for fresh rodent signs
    D. a binder should also be used to aid in mixing

TEST 2

Cylindrical surfaces are the most common form of finished surfaces found on machine parts, although flat surfaces are also very common; hence, many metal-cutting processes are for the purpose of producing either cylindrical or flat surfaces. The machines used for cylindrical or flat shapes may be, and often are, utilized also for forming the various irregular or special shapes required on many machine parts. Because of the prevalence of cylindrical and flat surfaces, the student of manufacturing practice should learn first about the machines and methods employed to produce these surfaces. The cylindrical surfaces may be internal as in holes and cylinders. Any one part may, of course, have cylindrical sections of different diameters and lengths and include flat ends or shoulders and, frequently, there is a threaded part or possibly some finished surface that is not circular in cross-section. The prevalence of cylindrical surfaces on machine parts explains why lathes are found in all machine shops. It is important to understand the various uses of the lathe because many of the operations are the same fundamentally as those performed on other types of machine tools.

1. According to the above paragraph, the most common form of finished surfaces found on machine parts is
    A.   cylindrical   B.   elliptical   C.   flat   D.   square

    1._____

2. According to the above paragraph, any one part of cylindrical surfaces may Have
    A.   chases   B.   shoulders   C.   keyways   D.   splines

    2._____

3. According to the above paragraph, lathes are found in all machine shops because cylindrical surfaces on machine parts are
    A.   scarce   B.   internal   C.   common   D.   external

    3._____

4. As used in the above paragraph, the word *processes* means
    A.   operations   B.   purposes   C.   devices   D.   tools

    4._____

Questions 5-6.

The principle of interchangeability requires manufacture to such specification that component parts of a device may be selected at random and assembled to fit and operate satisfactorily. Interchangeable manufacture, therefore, requires that parts be made to definite limits of error, and to fit gages instead of mating parts. Interchange-ability does not necessarily involve a high degree of precision; stove lids, for example, are interchangeable but are not particularly accurate, and carriage bolts and nuts are not precision products but are completely interchangeable. Interchangeability may be employed in unit-production as well as mass-production systems of manufacture.

5. According to the above paragraph, in order for parts to be interchangeable, they must be
    A.   precision-machined   B.   selectively-assembled
    C.   mass-produced   D.   made to fit gages

    5._____

6. According to the above paragraph, carriage bolts are interchangeable because they are

    A. precision-made   B. sized to specific tolerances
    C. individually matched products
    D. produced in small units

6.___

Questions 7-9.

The soda-acid fire extinguisher is the commonest type of water-solution extinguisher in which pressure is used to expel the water. The chemicals used are sodium bicarbonate (baking soda) and sulfuric acid. The sodium bicarbonate is dissolved in water, and this solution is the extinguishing agent. The extinguishing value of the stream is that of an equal quantity of water.

7. According to the above paragraph, the soda-acid extinguisher, compared to others of the same type, is the

    A. most widely used
    B. most effective in putting out fire
    C. cheapest to operate   D. easiest to operate

7.___

8. In the soda-acid extinguisher, the fire is put out by a solution of sodium bicardonate *and*

    A. sulfuric acid   B. baking soda
    C. soda-acid   D. water

8.___

9. According to the above paragraph, the sodium bicarbonate solution, compared to water, is

    A. more effective in putting out fires
    B. less effective in putting out fires
    C. equally effective in putting out fires
    D. more or less effective, depending upon the type of fire

9.___

Questions 10-12.

Some gases which may be inhaled have an irritant effect on the respiratory tract. Among them are ammonia fumes, hydrogen sulfide, nitrous fumes, and phosgene. Persons who have been exposed to irritant gases must lie down at once and keep absolutely quiet until the doctor arrives. The action of some of these gases may be delayed, and at first the fictim may show few or no symptoms.

10. According to the above paragraph, the part of the body that is most affected by irritant gases is the

    A. heart   B. lungs   C. skin   D. nerves

10.__

11. According to the above paragraph, a person who has inhaled an irritant gas should be

    A. given artificial respiration   B. made to rest
    C. wrapped in blankets   D. made to breathe smelling salts

11.__

12. A person is believed to have come in contact with an irritant gas but he does   12._____
    not become sick immediately. According to the above paragraph, we may
    conclude that the person
    A. did not really come in contact with the gas
    B. will become sick later
    C. came in contact with a small amount of gas
    D. may possibly become sick later

Questions 13-17.

At one time people thought that in the interview designed primarily to obtain
information, the interviewer had to resort to clever and subtle lines of questioning in order
to accomplish his ends.   Some people still believe that this is necessary, but it is not so.
An example of the "tricky" approach may be seen in the work of a recent study.   The
study deals with materials likely to be buried beneath deep defenses.   Interviewers
utilized methods of questioning which, in effect, trapped the interviewee and destroyed
his defenses.   Doubtless, these methods succeeded in bringing out items of
information which straightforward questions would have missed.   Whether they missed
more information than they obtained and whether they obtained the most important facts,
must remain unanswered questions.   In defense of the "clever" approach, it is often said
that, in many situations, the interviewee is motivated to conceal information or to distort
what he chooses to report.

Technically, it is likely that a highly skilled interviewer can, given the time and the
inclination, penetrate the interviewee's defenses and get information which the latter
intended to keep hidden. It is unlikely that the interviewer could successfully elicit all of
the information that might be relevant.   If, for example, he found that an applicant for
financial assistance was heavily in debt to gamblers, he might not care about getting any
other information.   There are situations in which one item, if answered in the "wrong"
way, is enough. Ordinarily, this is not true.   The usual situation is that there are many
considerations and that the plus and minus features must be weighed before a decision
may be made.   It is therefore important to obtain complete information.

13. According to the above passage, it was generally believed that an interviewer   13._____
    would have difficulty in obtaining the information he sought from a person if he
    A. were tricky in his methods
    B. were open and frank in his approach
    C. were clever in his questioning
    D. utilized carefully prepared questions

14. The passage does NOT reveal whether the type of questions used   14._____
    A. trapped those being interviewed
    B. elicited facts which an open method of questioning might miss
    C. elicited the most important facts that were sought
    D. covered matters which those interviewed were reluctant to talk about
       openly

15. An argument in favor of the "tricky" or "clever" interviewing technique is that,   15._____
    unless this approach is used, the person interviewed will *NOT*
    A. offer to furnish all pertinent information
    B. answer questions concerning routine data
    C. clearly understand what is being sought
    D. want to continue the interview

16. According to the above passage, in favorable circumstances, a talented   16.__
interviewer would be able to obtain from the person interviewed information
   A. which the person regards as irrelevant
   B. which the person intends to conceal
   C. about the person's family background
   D. which the person would normally have forgotten

17. According to the above passage, a highly skilled interviewer should   17.__
concentrate, in most cases, on getting
   A. one outstanding fact about the interviewee which would do away with
      the need for prolonged questioning
   B. facts which the interviewee wanted to conceal because these would
      be the most relevant in making a decision
   C. all the facts so that he can consider their relative values before
      reaching any conclusion
   D. information about any bad habits of the interviewee, such as gambling,
      which would make further questioning unnecessary

Questions 18-22.

For a period of nearly fifteen years, beginning in the mid-1950's, higher
education sustained a phenomenal rate of growth.   The factors principally responsible
were continuing improvement in the rate of college entrance by high school graduates, a
50-percent increase in the size of the college-age (eighteen to twenty-one) group, and –
until about 1967 – a rapid expansion of university research activity supported by the
federal government.

Today, as one looks ahead fifteen years to the year 2020, it is apparent that
each of these favorable stimuli will either be abated or turn into a negative factor.   The
rate of growth of the college-age group has already diminished, and from 2010 to 2015
the size of the college-age group will shrink annually almost as fast as it grew from 1965
to 1970.   From 2015 to 2020, this annual decrease will slow down so that by 2020 the
age-group will be about the same size as it was in 2019.   This substantial net decrease
in the size of the college-age group over the next fifteen years will dramatically affect
college enrollments since, currently, 83 percent of undergraduates are twenty-one and
under, and another 11 percent are twenty-two to twenty-four.

18. Which one of the following factors is NOT mentioned in the above passage as   18.__
contributing to the high rate of growth of higher education?
   A. A large increase in the size of the eighteen to twenty-one age group
   B. The equalization of educational opportunities among socio-economic
      groups
   C. The federal budget impact on research and development spending in
      the higher education sector
   D. The increasing rate at which high-school graduates enter college

19. Based on the information in the above passage, the size of the college-age   19.__
group in 2020 will be
   A. larger than it was in 2019
   B. larger than it was in 2005
   C. smaller than it was in 2015
   D. about the same as it was in 2010

20. According to the above passage, the tremendous rate of growth of higher   20._____
    education started around
        A.   1950   B.   1955   C.   1960   D.   1965

21. The percentage of undergraduates who are over age 25 is, most nearly,   21._____
        A.   6%   B.   8%   C.   11%   D.   17%

22. Which one of the following conclusions can be substantiated by the   22._____
    information given in the above passage?   The
        A.   college-age group will be about the same size in 2010 as it was in
             1965
        B.   annual decrease in the size of the college-age group from 2010 to
             2015 will be about the same as the annual increase from 1965 to 1970
        C.   overall decrease in the size of the college-age group from 2010 to
             2015 will be followed by an overall increase in its size from 2015 to
             2020
        D.   size of the college-age group will decrease at a fairly constant rate
             from 2005 to 2020

Questions 23-25.

    A fire of undetermined origin started in the warehouse shed of a flour mill.
Although there was some delay in notifying the fire department, they practically
succeeded in bringing the fire under control when a series of dust explosions occurred
which caused the fire to spread and the main building was destroyed.   The fire
department's efforts were considerably handicapped because it was undermanned, and
the water pressure in the vicinity was inadequate.

23. From the information contained in the above paragraph, it is *MOST* accurate   23._____
    to state that the cause of the fire was
        A.   suspicious   B.   unknown   C.   accidental
        D.   arson   E.   spontaneous combustion

24. In the fire described above, the *MOST* important cause of the fire spreading   24._____
    to the main building was the
        A.   series of dust explosions
        B.   delay in notifying the fire department
        C.   inadequate water pressure   D.   lack of manpower
        D.   wooden construction of the building

25. In the fire described above, the fire department's efforts were handicapped   25._____
    CHIEFLY by
        A.   poor leadership   B.   outdated apparatus
        C.   uncooperative company employees
        D.   insufficient water pressure   E.   poorly trained men

Questions 26-30.

    Upon the death of a member or former member of the retirement system there
shall be paid to his estate, or to the person he had nominated by written designation, his
accumulated deductions.   In addition, if he is a member who is in city service, there shall
be paid a sum consisting of: an amount equal to the compensation he earned while a

member during the three months immediately preceding his death, or, if the total number of years of allowable service exceeds five there shall be paid an amount equal to the compensation he earned while a member during the six months immediately preceding his death; and the reserve-for-increased-take-home-pay, if any.

Payment for the expense of burial, not exceeding two hundred and fifty dollars, may be made to a relative or friend who, in the absence or failure of the designated beneficiary, assumes this responsibility.

Until the first retirement benefit payment has been made, where a member has not selected an option, the member will be considered to be in city service, and the death benefits provided above will be paid instead of the retirement allowance. The member, or upon his death, his designated beneficiary, may provide that the actuarial equivalent of the benefit otherwise payable in a lump sum shall be paid in the form of an annuity payable in installments; the amount of such annuity is determined at the time of the member's death on the basis of the age of the beneficiary at that time.

26. Suppose that a member who has applied for retirement benefits without selecting an option dies before receiving any payments. According to the information in the above passage, this member's beneficiary would be entitled to receive
    A. an annuity based on the member's age at the time of his death
    B. a death benefit only
    C. the member's retirement allowance only
    D. the member's retirement allowance, plus a death-benefit payment in a lump sum

26.___

27. Suppose that a member died on June 15, 2007, while still in city service. He Had joined the retirement system in March 1990. During the year preceding his death, he earned $75,000. Based on the information in the above passage, the designated beneficiary of this member would be entitled to receive all of the following *EXCEPT*
    A. a payment of $37,500
    B. payment of burial expense up to $250
    C. the member's accumulated deductions
    D. the reserve-for-increased-take-home-pay, if any

27.___

28. According to the information in the above passage, the amount of the benefit payable upon the death of a member is based, in part, on the
    A. length of city service during which the deceased person was a member
    B. number of beneficiaries the deceased member had nominated
    C. percent of the deceased member's deductions for social security
    D. type of retirement plan to which the deceased member belonged

28.___

29. According to the information in the above passage, which one of the following statements concerning the payment of death benefits is *CORRECT?*
    A. In order for a death benefit to be paid, the deceased member must have previously nominated, in writing, someone to receive the benefit
    B. Death benefits are paid upon the death of members who are in city service
    C. A death benefit must be paid in one lump sum
    D. When a retired person dies, his retirement allowance is replaced by a death-benefit payment

29.___

30. According to the information in the above passage, the   30._____
amount of annuity payments made to a beneficiary in monthly installments in lieu
of a lump-sum payment is determined by the
    A.   length of member's service at the time of his death
    B.   age of the beneficiary at the time of the member's death
    C.   member's age at retirement
    D.   member's age at the time of his death

_____

KEYS (CORRECT ANSWERS)

TEST 1					TEST 2			
1.	D	11.	D		1.	A	16.	B
2.	C	12.	C		2.	B	17.	C
3.	B	13.	D		3.	C	18.	B
4.	A	14.	B		4.	A	19.	C
5.	B	15.	A		5.	D	20.	B
6.	B	16.	A		6.	B	21.	A
7.	A	17.	C		7.	A	22.	B
8.	D	18.	D		8.	D	23.	B
9.	D	19.	C		9.	C	24.	A
10.	A	20.	D		10.	B	25.	D
		21	B		11.	B	26.	B
		22	B		12.	D	27.	B
		23.	C		13.	B	28.	A
		24.	C		14.	C	29.	B
		25.	D		15.	A	30.	B

_____

PREPARING WRITTEN MATERIAL
EXAMINATION SECTION

DIRECTIONS FOR TESTS 1-8:
Each of the sentences in the Tests that follow may be classified under one of the following four categories:
A. *Faulty* because of incorrect grammar or word usage
B. *Faulty* because of incorrect punctuation
C. *Faulty* because of incorrect capitalization or incorrect spelling
D. *Correct*

Examine each sentence carefully to determine under which of the above four options it is best classified. Then, in the space to the right, print the capital letter preceding the option which is the best of the four suggested above.

(Note that each faulty sentence contains but one type of error. Consider a sentence to be correct if it contains none of the types of errors mentioned, even though there may be other correct ways of expressing the same thought.)

TEST 1

1. He sent the notice to the clerk who you hired yesterday.   1. ...
2. It must be admitted, however that you were not informed of this change.   2. ...
3. Only the employees who have served in this grade for at least two years are eligible for promotion.   3. ...
4. The work was divided equally between she and Mary.   4. ...
5. He thought that you were not available at that time.   5. ...
6. When the messenger returns; please give him this package.   6. ...
7. The new secretary prepared, typed, addressed, and delivered, the notices.   7. ...
8. Walking into the room, his desk can be seen at the rear.   8. ...
9. Although John has worked here longer than She, he produces a smaller amount of work.   9. ...
10. She said she could of typed this report yesterday.   10. ...
11. Neither one of these procedures are adequate for the efficient performance of this task.   11. ...
12. The typewriter is the tool of the typist; the cash register, the tool of the cashier.   12. ...
13. "The assignment must be completed as soon as possible" said the supervisor.   13. ...
14. As you know, office handbooks are issued to all new Employees.   14. ...
15. Writing a speech is sometimes easier than to deliver it before an audience.   15. ...
16. Mr. Brown our accountant, will audit the accounts next week.   16. ...
17. Give the assignment to whomever is able to do it most efficiently.   17. ...
18. The supervisor expected either your or I to file these reports.   18. ...

TEST 2

1. The fire apparently started in the storeroom, which is usually locked.   1. ...

1

2. On approaching the victim two bruises were noticed by   2. ...
   this officer.
3. The officer, who was there examined the report with great   3. ...
   care.
4. Each employee in the office had a seperate desk.   4. ...
5. All employees including members of the clerical staff,   5. ...
   were invited to the lecture.
6. The suggested Procedure is similar to the one now in use.   6. ...
7. No one was more pleased with the new procedure than the   7. ...
   chauffeur.
8. He tried to persaude her to change the procedure.   8. ...
9. The total of the expenses charged to petty cash were high.   9. ...
10. An understanding between him and I was finally reached.   10. ...

TEST 3

1. They told both he and I that the prisoner had escaped.   1. ...
2. Any superior officer, who, disregards the just complaints   2. ...
   of his subordinates, is remiss in the performance of his
   duty.
3. Only those members of the national organization who resided 3. ...
   in the Middle West attended the conference in Chicago.
4. We told him to give the investigation assignment to who-   4. ...
   ever was available.
5. Please do not disappoint and embarass us by not appearing   5. ...
   in court.
6. Although the officer's speech proved to be entertaining,   6. ...
   the topic was not relevent to the main theme of the conference.
7. In February all new officers attended a training course   7. ...
   in which they were learned in their principal duties and
   the fundamental operating procedures of the department.
8. I personally seen inmate Jones threaten inmates Smith and   8. ...
   Green with bodily harm if they refused to participate in
   the plot.
9. To the layman, who on a chance visit to the prison ob-   9. ...
   serves everything functioning smoothly, the maintenance
   of prison discipline may seem to be a relatively easily
   realizable objective.
10. The prisoners in cell block fourty were forbidden to sit   10. ...
    on the cell cots during the recreation hour.

TEST 4

1. I cannot encourage you any.   1. ...
2. You always look well in those sort of clothes.   2. ...
3. Shall we go to the park?   3. ...
4. The man whome he introduced was Mr. Carey.   4. ...
5. She saw the letter laying here this morning.   5. ...
6. It should rain before the Afternoon is over.   6. ...
7. They have already went home.   7. ...
8. That Jackson will be elected is evident.   8. ...
9. He does not hardly approve of us.   9. ...
10. It was he, who won the prize.   10. ...

TEST 5

1. Shall we go to the park.   1. ...
2. They are, alike, in this particular.   2. ...
3. They gave the poor man sume food when he knocked on the   3. ...
   door.
4. I regret the loss caused by the error.   4. ...
5. The students' will have a new teacher.   5. ...
6. They sweared to bring out all the facts.   6. ...
7. He decided to open a branch store on 33rd street.   7. ...
8. His speed is equal and more than that of a racehorse.   8. ...
9. He felt very warm on that Summer day.   9. ...
10. He was assisted by his friend, who lives in the next house.10. ...

TEST 6

1. The climate of New York is colder than California.   1. ...
2. I shall wait for you on the corner.   2. ...
3. Did we see the boy who, we think, is the leader.   3. ...
4. Being a modest person, John seldom talks about his in-   4. ...
   vention.
5. The gang is called the smith street boys.   5. ...
6. He seen the man break into the store.   6. ...
7. We expected to lay still there for quite a while.   7. ...
8. He is considered to be the Leader of his organization.   8. ...
9. Although I recieved an invitation, I won't go.   9. ...
10. The letter must be here some place.   10. ...

TEST 7

1. I though it to be he.   1. ...
2. We expect to remain here for a long time.   2. ...
3. The committee was agreed.   3. ...
4. Two-thirds of the building are finished.   4. ...
5. The water was froze.   5. ...
6. Everyone of the salesmen must supply their own car.   6. ...
7. Who is the author of Gone With the Wind?   7. ...
8. He marched on and declaring that he would never surrender.   8. ...
9. Who shall I say called?   9. ...
10. Everyone has left but they.   10. ...

TEST 8

1. Who did we give the order to?   1. ...
2. Send your order in immediately.   2. ...
3. I believe I paid the Bill.   3. ...
4. I have not met but one person.   4. ...
5. Why aren't Tom, and Fred, going to the dance?   5. ...
6. What reason is there for him not going?   6. ...
7. The seige of Malta was a tremendous event.   7. ...
8. I was there yesterday I assure you.   8. ...
9. Your ukelele is better than mine.   9. ...
10. No one was there only Mary.   10. ...

TEST 9

DIRECTIONS FOR TEST 9:
   In each of the following groups of sentences, one of the four sentences is faulty in grammar, punctuation, or capitalization. Select the incorrect sentence in each case.

1. A. If you had stood at home and done your homework, you   1. ...
       would not have failed in arithmetic.
    B. Her affected manner annoyed every member of the audience.
    C. How will the new law affect our income taxes?
    D. The plants were not affected by the long, cold winter,
       but they succumbed to the drought of summer.
2. A. He is one of the most able men who have been in the   2. ...
       Senate.
    B. It is he who is to blame for the lamentable mistake.
    C. Haven't you a helpful suggestion to make at this time?
    D. The money was robbed from the blind man's cup.
3. A. The amount of children in this school is steadily in-   3. ...
       creasing.
    B. After taking an apple from the table, she went out to play.
    C. He borrowed a dollar from me.
    D. I had hoped my brother would arrive before me.
4. A. Whom do you think I hear from every week?
    B. Who do you think is the right man for the job?   4. ...
    C. Who do you think I found in the room?
    D. He is the man whom we considered a good candidate for
       the presidency.
5. A. Quietly the puppy laid down before the fireplace.   5. ...
    B. You have made your bed; now lie in it.
    C. I was badly sunburned because I had lain too long in the
       sun.
    D. I laid the doll on the bed and left the room.

KEYS (CORRECT ANSWERS)

TEST 1		TEST 2	TEST 3	TEST 4	TEST 5
1. A	10. A	1. D	1. A	1. A	1. B
2. B	11. A	2. A	2. B	2. A	2. B
3. D	12. C	3. B	3. C	3. D	3. C
4. A	13. B	4. C	4. D	4. C	4. D
5. D	14. C	5. B	5. C	5. A	5. B
6. B	15. A	6. C	6. C	6. C	6. A
7. B	16. B	7. D	7. A	7. A	7. C
8. A	17. A	8. C	8. A	8. D	8. A
9. C	18. A	9. A	9. D	9. A	9. C
		10. A	10. C	10. B	10. D

TEST 6	TEST 7	TEST 8	TEST 9
1. A	1. A	1. A	1. A
2. D	2. D	2. D	2. D
3. B	3. D	3. C	3. A
4. D	4. A	4. A	4. C
5. C	5. A	5. B	5. A
6. A	6. A	6. A	
7. A	7. B	7. C	
8. C	8. A	8. B	
9. C	9. D	9. C	
10. A	10. D	10. A	

PREPARING WRITTEN MATERIAL

PARAGRAPH REARRANGEMENT
COMMENTARY

The sentences which follow are in scrambled order. You are to rearrange them in proper order and indicate the letter choice containing the correct answer at the space at the right.

Each group of sentences in this section is actually a paragraph presented in scrambled order. Each sentence in the group has a place in that paragraph; no sentence is to be left out. You are to read each group of sentences and decide upon the best order in which to put the sentences so as to form as well-organized paragraph.

The questions in this section measure the ability to solve a problem when all the facts relevant to its solution are not given.

More specifically, certain positions of responsibility and authority require the employee to discover connections between events sometimes, apparently, unrelated. In order to do this, the employee will find it necessary to correctly infer that unspecified events have probably occurred or are likely to occur. This ability becomes especially important when action must be taken on incomplete information.

Accordingly, these questions require competitors to choose among several suggested alternatives, each of which presents a different sequential arrangement of the events. Competitors must choose the MOST logical of the suggested sequences.

In order to do so, they may be required to draw on general knowledge to infer missing concepts or events that are essential to sequencing the given events. Competitors should be careful to infer only what is essential to the sequence. The plausibility of the wrong alternatives will always require the inclusion of unlikely events or of additional chains of events which are NOT essential to sequencing the given events.

It's very important to remember that you are looking for the best of the four possible choices, and that the best choice of all may not even be one of the answers you're given to choose from.

There is no one right way to these problems. Many people have found it helpful to first write out the order of the sentences, as they would have arranged them, on their scrap paper before looking at the possible answers. If their optimum answer is there, this can save them some time. If it isn't, this method can still give insight into solving the problem. Others find it most helpful to just go through each of the possible choices, contrasting each as they go along. You should use whatever method feels comfortable, and works, for you.

While most of these types of questions are not that difficult, we've added a higher percentage of the difficult type, just to give you more practice. Usually there are only one or two questions on this section that contain such subtle distinctions that you're unable to answer confidently, and you then may find yourself stuck deciding between two possible choices, neither of which you're sure about.

———

EXAMINATION SECTION
TEST 1

DIRECTIONS: The sentences that follow are in scrambled order. You are to rearrange them in proper order and indicate the letter choice containing the correct answer. *PRINT THE LETTER OF THE CORRECT ANSWER IN THE SPACE AT THE RIGHT.*

1.   Below are four statements labeled W., X., Y., and Z.   1._____
    W.   He was a strict and fanatic drillmaster.
    X.   The word is always used in a derogatory sense and generally shows resentment and anger on the part of the user.
    Y.   It is from the name of this Frenchman that we derive our English word, martinet.
    Z.   Jean Martinet was the Inspector-General of Infantry during the reign of King Louis XIV.
    The *PROPER* order in which these sentences should be placed in a paragraph is:

    A. X, Z, W, Y   B. X, Z, Y, W   C. Z, W, Y, X   D. Z, Y, W, X

2.   In the following paragraph, the sentences which are numbered, have been jumbled.   2._____
    1.   Since then it has undergone changes.
    2.   It was incorporated in 1955 under the laws of the State of New York.
    3.   Its primary purpose, a cleaner city, has, however, remained the same.
    4.   The Citizens Committee works in cooperation with the Mayor's Inter-departmental Committee for a Clean City.
    The order in which these sentences should be arranged to form a well-organized paragraph is:

    A. 2, 4, 1, 3   B. 3, 4, 1, 2   C. 4, 2, 1, 3   D. 4, 3, 2, 1

Questions 3-5.

DIRECTIONS: The sentences listed below are part of a meaningful paragraph but they are not given in their proper order. You are to decide what would be the *best order* in which to put the sentences so as to form a well-organized paragraph. Each sentence has a place in the paragraph; there are no extra sentences. You are then to answer questions 3 to 5 inclusive on the basis of your rearrangements of these secrambled sentences into a properly organized paragraph.

In 1887 some insurance companies organized an Inspection Department to advise their clients on all phases of fire prevention and protection. Probably this has been due to the smaller annual fire losses in Great Britain than in the United States. It tests various fire prevention devices and appliances and determines manufacturing hazards and their safeguards. Fire research began earlier in the United States and is more advanced than in Great Britain. Later they established a laboratory specializing in electrical, mechanical, hydraulic, and chemical fields.

3. When the five sentences are arranged in proper order, the paragraph starts with the sentence which begins   3._

    A.   "In 1887 ..."   B.   "Probably this ..."   C.   "It tests ..."
    D.   "Fire research ..."   E.   "Later they ..."

4. In the last sentence listed above, "they" refers to   4._

    A.   insurance companies
    B.   the United States and Great Britain
    C.   the Inspection Department
    D.   clients
    E.   technicians

5. When the above paragraph is properly arranged, it ends with the words   5._

    A.   "... and protection."   B.   "... the United States."
    C.   "... their safeguards."   D.   "... in Great Britain."
    E.   "... chemical fields."

KEY (CORRECT ANSWERS)

    1. C
    2. C
    3. D
    4. A
    5. C

TEST 2

DIRECTIONS: In each of the questions numbered 1 through 5, several sentences are given. For each question, choose as your answer the group of numbers that represents the *most logical* order of these sentences if they were arranged in paragraph form. *PRINT THE LETTER OF THE CORRECT ANSWER IN THE SPACE AT THE RIGHT.*

1. 1. It is established when one shows that the landlord has prevented the tenant's enjoyment of his interest in the property leased.

    2. Constructive eviction is the result of a breach of the covenant of quiet enjoyment implied in all leases.

    3. In some parts of the United States, it is not complete until the tenant vacates within a reasonable time.

    4. Generally, the acts must be of such serious and permanent character as to deny the tenant the enjoyment of his possessing rights.

    5. In this event, upon abandonment of the premises, the tenant's liability for that ceases.

    The CORRECT answer is:

    A. 2, 1, 4, 3, 5   B. 5, 2, 3, 1, 4   C. 4, 3, 1, 2, 5
    D. 1, 3, 5, 4, 2

1.____

2. 1. The powerlessness before private and public authorities that is the typical experience of the slum tenant is reminiscent of the situation of blue-collar workers all through the nineteenth century.

    2. Similarly, in recent years, this chapter of history has been reopened by anti-poverty groups which have attempted to organize slum tenants to enable them to bargain collectively with their landlords about the conditions of their tenancies.

    3. It is familiar history that many of the workers remedied their condition by joining together and presenting their demands collectively.

    4. Like the workers, tenants are forced by the conditions of modern life into substantial dependence on these who possess great political arid economic power.

    5. What's more, the very fact of dependence coupled with an absence of education and self-confidence makes them hesitant and unable to stand up for what they need from those in power.

    The CORRECT answer is:

    A. 5, 4, 1, 2, 3   B. 2, 3, 1, 5, 4   C. 3, 1, 5, 4, 2
    D. 1, 4, 5, 3, 2

2.____

3. 1. A railroad, for example, when not acting as a common carrier may contract; away responsibility for its own negligence.

    2. As to a landlord, however, no decision has been found relating to the legal effect of a clause shifting the statutory duty of repair to the tenant.

    3. The courts have not passed on the validity of clauses relieving the landlord of this duty and liability.

    4. They have, however, upheld the validity of exculpatory clauses in other types of contracts.

    5. Housing regulations impose a duty upon the landlord to maintain leased premises in safe condition.

3.____

6. As another example, a bailee may limit his liability except for gross negligence, willful acts, or fraud.

The CORRECT answer is:

A. 2, 1, 6, 4, 3, 5   B. 1, 3, 4, 5, 6, 2   C. 3, 5, 1, 4, 2, 6
D. 5, 3, 4, 1, 6, 2

4. 1. Since there are only samples in the building, retail or consumer sales are generally eschewed by mart occupants, and, in some instances, rigid controls are maintained to limit entrance to the mart only to those persons engaged in retailing.
2. Since World War I, in many larger cities, there has developed a new type of property, called the mart building.
3. It can, therefore, be used by wholesalers and jobbers for the display of sample merchandise.
4. This type of building is most frequently a multi-storied, finished interior property which is a cross between a retail arcade and a loft building.
5. This limitation enables the mart occupants to ship the orders from another location after the retailer or dealer makes his selection from the samples.

The CORRECT answer is:

A. 2, 4, 3, 1, 5   B. 4, 3, 5, 1, 2   C. 1, 3, 2, 4, 5
D. 1, 4, 2, 3, 5

5. 1. In general, staff-line friction reduces the distinctive contribution of staff personnel.
2. The conflicts, however, introduce an uncontrolled element into the managerial system.
3. On the other hand, the natural resistance of the line to staff innovations probably usefully restrains over-eager efforts to apply untested procedures on a large scale.
4. Under such conditions, it is difficult to know when valuable ideas are being sacrificed.
5. The relatively weak position of staff, requiring accommodation to the line, tends to restrict their ability to engage .in free, experimental innovation.

The CORRECT answer is:

A. 4, 2, 3, 1, 3   B. 1, 5, 3, 2, 4   C. 5, 3, 1, 2, 4
D. 2, 1, 4, 5, 3

KEY (CORRECT ANSWERS)

1. A
2. D
3. D
4. A
5. B

TEST 3

DIRECTIONS: Questions 1 through 4 consist of six sentences which can be arranged in a logical sequence. For each question, select the choice which places the numbered sentences in the *most logical* sequence. *PRINT THE LETTER OF THE CORRECT ANSWER IN THE SPACE AT THE RIGHT.*

1.   1.   The burden of proof as to each issue is determined before trial and remains upon the same party throughout the trial.

         2.   The jury is at liberty to believe one witness' testimony as against a number of contradictory witnesses.

         3.   In a civil case, the party bearing the burden of proof is required to prove his contention by a fair preponderance of the evidence.

         4.   However, it must be noted that a fair preponderance of evidence does not necessarily mean a greater number of witnesses.

         5.   The burden of proof is the burden which rests upon one of the parties to an action to persuade the trier of the facts, generally the jury, that a proposition he asserts is true.

         6.   If the evidence is equally balanced, or if it leaves the jury in such doubt as to be unable to decide the controversy either way, judgment must be given against the party upon whom the burden of proof rests.

      The CORRECT answer is:

      A. 3, 2, 5, 4, 1, 6   B. 1, 2, 6, 5, 3, 4   C. 3, 4, 5, 1, 2, 6
      D. 5, 1, 3, 6, 4, 2

1.____

2.   1.   If a parent is without assets and is unemployed, he cannot be convicted of the crime of non-support of a child.

         2.   The term "sufficient ability" has been held to mean sufficient financial ability.

         3.   It does not matter if his unemployment is by choice or unavoidable circumstances.

         4.   If he fails to take any steps at all, he may be liable to prosecution for endangering the welfare of a child.

         5.   Under the penal law, a parent is responsible for the support of his minor child only if the parent is "of sufficient ability."

         6.   An indigent parent may meet his obligation by borrowing money or by seeking aid under the provisions of the Social Welfare Law.

      The CORRECT answer is:

      A. 6, 1, 5, 3, 2, 4   B. 1, 3, 5, 2, 4, 6   C. 5, 2, 1, 3, 6, 4
      D. 1, 6, 4, 5, 2, 3

2.____

3.
1. Consider, for example, the case of a rabble rouser who urges a group of twenty people to go out and break the windows of a nearby factory.
2. Therefore, the law fills the indicated gap with the crime of inciting to riot."
3. A person is considered guilty of inciting to riot when he urges ten or more persons to engage in tumultuous and violent conduct of a kind likely to create public alarm.
4. However, if he has not obtained the cooperation of at least four people, he cannot be charged with unlawful assembly.
5. The charge of inciting to riot was added to the law to cover types of conduct which cannot be classified as either the crime of "riot" or the crime of "unlawful assembly."
6. If he acquires the acquiescence of at least four of them, he is guilty of unlawful assembly even if the project does not materialize.

The CORRECT answer is:

A. 3, 5, 1, 6, 4, 2   B. 5, 1, 4, 6, 2, 3   C. 3, 4, 1, 5, 2, 6
D. 5, 1, 4, 6, 3, 2

4.
1. If, however, the rebuttal evidence presents an issue of credibility, it is for the jury to determine whether the presumption has, in fact, been destroyed.
2. Once sufficient evidence to the contrary is introduced, the presumption disappears from the trial.
3. The effect of a presumption is to place the burden upon the adversary to come forward with evidence to rebut the presumption.
4. When a presumption is overcome and ceases to exist in the case, the fact or facts which gave rise to the presumption still remain.
5. Whether a presumption has been overcome is ordinarily a question for the court.
6. Such information may furnish a basis for a logical inference.

The CORRECT answer is:

A. 4, 6, 2, 5, 1, 3   B. 3, 2, 5, 1, 4, 6   C. 5, 3, 6, 4, 2, 1
D. 5, 4, 1, 2, 6, 3

_____

KEY (CORRECT ANSWERS)

1. D
2. C
3. A
4. B

_____

INTERPRETING STATISTICAL DATA
GRAPHS, CHARTS AND TABLES

DIRECTIONS: Each question or incomplete statement is followed by
several suggested answers or completions. Select the
one that BEST answers the question or completes the
statement. *PRINT THE LETTER OF THE CORRECT ANSWER IN
THE SPACE AT THE RIGHT.*

TEST 1

1. The following chart shows the number of persons employed   1.___
    in a certain industry for each year from 1977 through 1982.

	Thousands of Employees
1977	5.7
1978	6.8
1979	7.0
1980	7.1
1981	7.4
1982	6.4

In making a forecast of future trends, the one of the
following steps which should be taken FIRST is to
   A. take the six-year average
   B. fit a curvilinear trend to the data
   C. fit a straight line, omitting 1982 as an *outlier*, i.e.,
      as an unusually low reading
   D. check on what happened to the industry in 1982

2. Of the following concepts, the one which CANNOT be   2.___
    represented suitably by a pie chart is
    A. percent shares
    B. shares in absolute units
    C. time trends
    D. successive totals over time, with their shares

3. A pictogram is ESSENTIALLY another version of a(n) _____   3.___
    chart.
       A. plain bar   B. component bar
       C. pie   D. area

4. A time series for a certain cost is presented in a graph.   4.___
    It is drawn so that the vertical (cost) axis starts at a
    point well above zero.
    This is a legitimate method of presentation for some
    purposes, but it may have the effect of
       A. hiding fixed components of the cost
       B. exaggerating changes which, in actual amounts, may
          be insignificant
       C. magnifying fixed components of the cost
       D. impairing correlation analysis

5. Certain budgetary data may be represented by bar, area   5
    or volume charts.
    Which one of the following BEST expresses the most
    appropriate order of usefulness?
    A. Descends from bar to volume and area charts, the
        last two being about the same
    B. Descends from volume to area to bar charts
    C. Depends on the nature of the data presented
    D. Descends from bar to area to volume charts

Questions 6-7.

DIRECTIONS: Questions 6 and 7 are to be answered on the basis of t
              layout below.

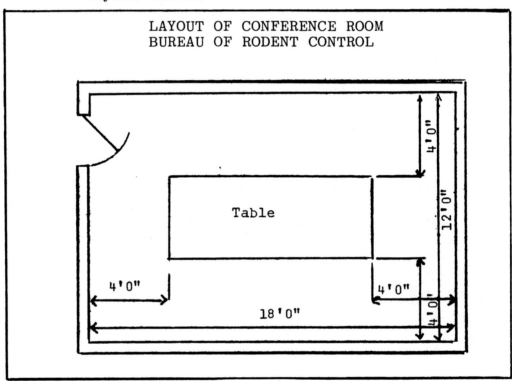

LAYOUT OF CONFERENCE ROOM
BUREAU OF RODENT CONTROL

6. The LARGEST number of persons that can be accommodated in   6
    the area shown in the layout is
    A. 16   B. 10   C. 8   D. 6

7. Assume that the Bureau's programs undergo expansion and   7
    the Director indicates that the feasibility of increasing
    the size of the conference room should be explored.
    For every two additional persons that are to be accommo-
    dated, the analyst should recommend that _____ be added
    to table length and _____ be added to room length.
    A. 2'-6"; 2'-6"   B. 5'-0"; 5'-0"
    C. 2'-6"; 5'-0"   D. 5'-0"; 2'-6"

Questions 8-9.

DIRECTIONS: Questions 8 and 9 are to be answered on the basis of the
              following groups, both of which depict the same informa-
              tion in different ways.
              The x and y axes in graphs A and B are not necessarily
              drawn in the same scale. The points along the curves
              on both graphs represent corresponding points and are
              the upper limits of class intervals.

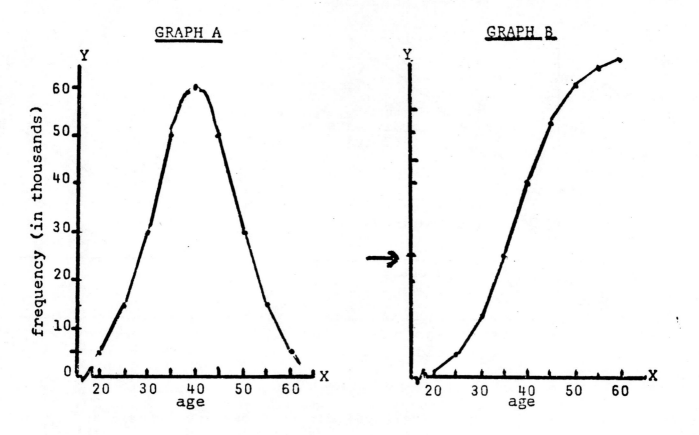

8.   The ordinate (y-axis) in graph B is   8.___
        A. frequency   B. cumulative frequency
        C. average frequency   D. log frequency

9.   The arrow on the y-axis in graph B indicates a particular   9.___
     number.
     That number is MOST NEARLY
        A. 100   B. 50,000   C. 100,000   D. 150,000

Questions 10-11.

DIRECTIONS: Questions 10 and 11 are to be answered on the basis of
the graphs below.

ROAD REPAIR COSTS IF PERFORMED BY
CITY STAFF OR AN OUTSIDE CONTRACTOR

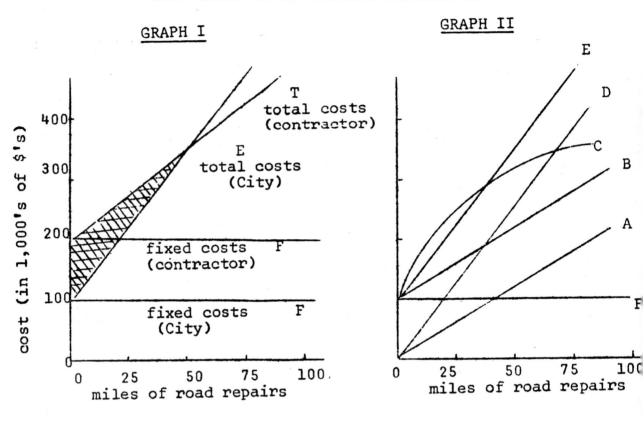

10.   In Graph I, the vertical distance between lines E and T   10
within the crosshatched area represents the _____ than
50 miles is performed by the city.
A. savings to the city if work of less
B. loss to the city if work of less
C. savings to the city if work of more
D. loss to the city if work of more

11.   Graph II is identical to Graph I except that contractor   11
costs have been eliminated. Total costs (line E) are
the sum of fixed costs (line F) and variable costs.
Variable costs are represented by line
A. A   B. B   C. C   D. D

Questions 12-13.

DIRECTIONS: Questions 12 and 13 are to be answered on the basis of
               the following chart.
               In a hypothetical problem involving four criteria and
               four alternatives, the following data have been
               assembled.

Cost Criterion	Effectiveness Criterion	Timing Criterion	Feasibility Criterion
Alternative A $500,000	50 units	3 months	probably feasible
Alternative B $300,000	100 units	6 months	probably feasible
Alternative C $400,000	50 units	12 months	probably infeasible
Alternative D $200,000	75 units	3 months	probably infeasible

12. On the basis of the above data, it appears that the one   12.____
     alternative which is dominated by another alternative is
     Alternative
          A. A   B. B   C. C   D. D

13. If the feasibility constraint is absolute and fixed, then   13.____
     the critical trade-off is between lower cost ____ on the
     other.
          A. on the one hand and faster timing and higher effective-
             ness
          B. and higher effectiveness on one hand and faster timing
          C. and faster timing on the one hand and higher effective-
             ness
          D. on the one hand and higher effectiveness

14. The following illustration depicts the structure of a   14
    municipal agency.

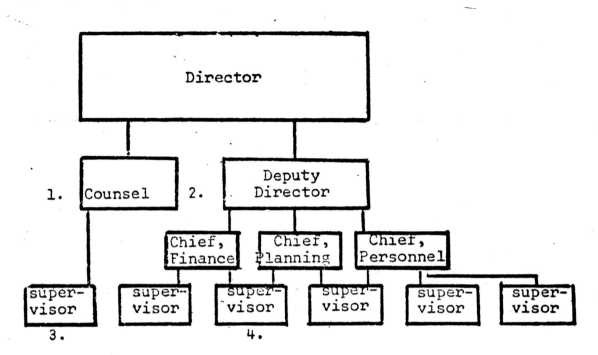

In the above illustration, which individual would generally
be expected to encounter the MOST difficulty in carrying
out his organizational functions?
A. 1   B. 2   C. 3   D. 4

Questions 15-16.

DIRECTIONS: Questions 15 and 16 are to be answered on the basis of
              the information given on the report forms pictured
              below and on the following page.

    Chart I and Chart II are parts of the Field Patrol Sheets of
two Parking Enforcement Agents. They show the number of violations
issued on a particular day. Chart III is the Tally Sheet for that
day prepared by the Senior Parking Enforcement Agent from the Field
Patrol Sheets of the entire squad.

CHART I

Area or Post	TYPE OF VIOLATION											
	Mtrs	B/S	D/P	Hyd	N/S	N/Sp	Taxi	Curb	N/P	Alt	Other	Total
19	2	3	2	2	3	3	0	1	1	5	1	23
21	4	0	2	0	1	2	2	0	5	9	1	26
Totals	6	3	4	2	4	5	2	1	6	14	2	49

2/4/76	100	PEA Browne	
Date	Badge	Signature	

TCB-61
Rev. 7/74   Checked by _____ Date _____

CHART II

Area or Post	TYPE OF VIOLATION											Total
	Mtrs	B/S	D/P	Hyd	N/S	N/Sp	Taxi	Curb	N/P	Alt	Other	
31	8	2	0	0	3	2	2	0	4	5	0	26
33	7	0	1	2	3	1	2	0	6	3	0	25
Totals	15	2	1	2	6	3	4	0	10	8	0	51

2/4/76	101	PEA Grey
Date	Badge	Signature

TCB-61
Rev. 7/74   Checked by _____   Date _____

CHART III

TRAFFIC CONTROL BUREAU
SENIORS TALLY SHEET   Enf. 23A

Name	Mtrs Ptld	Mtrs	Bus Stop	Dble Park	Hyd	No Stand	No Stop	Taxi Stand	Curb	No Park	Alt Park	Other	Total
een		18	2	3	1	6	0	0	0	4	10	1	45
owne		6	3	4	2	4	5	2	1	6	14	2	49
ite		12	0	0	0	2	1	1	0	8	8	1	33
ack		20	5	2	3	8	7	5	1	5	4	0	60
ey		15	2	1	2	9	3	4	0	10	8	0	51
dding		17	0	1	3	7	5	3	0	8	6	0	50
TOTAL		88	12	11	11	36	21	15	2	41	50	4	288

15. The Senior Parking Enforcement Agent who prepared Chart III   15.____
    made an error in transferring the violation totals from the
    Field Patrol Sheets to the Seniors Tally Sheet.
    Which one of the following PROPERLY describes the Tally
    Sheet entry if this error were corrected?
    Parking Enforcement Agent
      A. Browne's overall total of summonses issued would be 50
      B. Browne's total of summonses issued for Double-Parking
         violations would be 3

C. Grey's total number of summonses issued for meter violations would be 6
D. Grey's total number of summonses issued for No Standing violations would be 6

16. The parking enforcement agent who issued the MOST summonses 16.__ for bus stop and taxi stand violations is
    A. Black   B. Redding   C. White   D. Browne

17. During a period of probation in which records were kept 17.__ for 360 children fourteen to eighteen years of age, probation officers found that the group committed certain offenses, as shown in the following table:

I.Q.	No. of Offenders	No. of Offenses	Offenses Per Offender
61-80	125	338	2.7
81-100	160	448	2.8
101 & over	75	217	2.9

According to the foregoing data,
   A. the more intelligent offenders are no more law-abiding than, and perhaps not so law-abiding as, the dull offenders
   B. brighter offenders present no more difficult problems than less intelligent offenders
   C. the majority of this probation group is found to be above the average in intelligence of a normal group of young persons within this age range
   D. the relationship between the effectiveness of probation work and the number of offenders is in inverse ratio

18. 18.__

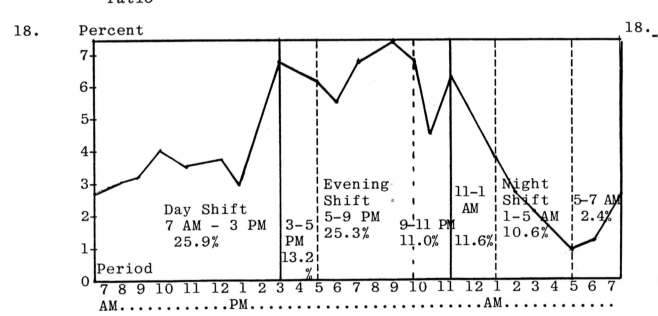

The percent for each hour is charted at the beginning of the hour. For example, 2.6% at the extreme left is for 7:00 A.M. to 7:59 A.M.

A certain police department has analyzed its need for police service and has computed the percentage distributions as shown on the chart on the preceding page. Despite good supervisory effort, there is a significant decrease in the amount of police service provided during the half-hour surrounding shift changes. The police commander wishes to minimize this effect.

To accomplish its objective, taking into account the distribution of need for police services, which one of the following is the BEST time for this department to schedule its three principal shift changes? (Assume 8-hour shifts.)
   A. 4:00 A.M., Noon, 8:00 P.M.
   B. 4:00 A.M., 1:00 P.M., 9:00 P.M.
   C. 6:00 A.M., 2:00 P.M., 10:00 P.M.
   D. 7:00 A.M., 3:00 P.M., 11:00 P.M.

19. An inspector on a painting contract has to keep records   19.___
on the progress of the work completed by a painting contractor.

The following is the progress of the work completed by a contractor at the end of 8 months.

Apartment Size	Estimated Number of Apartments	Number of Apartments Painted
3 rooms	120	100
4 rooms	160	140
5 rooms	120	40

The percentage of work completed on a room basis is MOST NEARLY
   A. 62%   B. 66%   C. 70%   D. 74%

20. Assume that an officer reported the following amounts of   20.___
toll monies collected during each day of a five-day period:

Tuesday	$3,247.50
Wednesday	$2,992.50
Thursday	$3,917.50
Friday	$4,862.50
Saturday	$1,675.00

The TOTAL amount of toll money collected during this period was
   A. $15,702.50   B. $16,485.00
   C. $16,695.00   D. $16,997.50

21. Suppose that during a two-hour period in a toll booth an   21.___
officer collected the following:

Type of Money	Number of Bills
$20 bills	2
$10 bills	5
$5 bills	23
$1 bills	269

The TOTAL amount of money the officer collected was
   A. $299   B. $464   C. $474   D. $501

Questions 22-23.

DIRECTIONS: Questions 22 and 23 are to be answered SOLELY on the b
of the information shown below which indicates the cha
for hospital services and physician services given in
hospital and a patient's annual income for each of fou
consecutive years.

Year	Patient's Annual Income	Charges for Hospital Services and Physician Services Given in a Hospital
1979	$15,000	$3,700
1980	$15,500	$3,990
1981	$21,500	$5,410
1982	$23,500	$5,775

22. A hospitalized patient may qualify for Medicaid benefits
when the charges for hospital services and for physician
services given in the hospital exceed 25 percent of the
patient's annual income.
According to the information shown above, the one of the
following that indicates ONLY those years in which the
patient qualifies for Medicaid benefits is
  A. 1980, 1981   B. 1979, 1980, 1982
  C. 1980, 1982   D. 1980, 1981, 1982

23. The one of the following that is the patient's average
annual income for the entire four-year period shown above
is MOST NEARLY
  A. $16,125   B. $16,375   C. $18,675   D. $18,875

Questions 24-25.

DIRECTIONS: Questions 24 and 25 are to be answered SOLELY on the
basis of the information shown below, which gives the
hospital bill and the amount paid by an Insurance Plar
for each of four patients.

Patient's Name	Hospital Bill	Amount Paid by the Insurance Plan Toward Hospital Bill
Mr. D. Harris	$ 8,753	$5,952
Mr. W. Smith	$ 4,504	$3,285
Mr. T. Jones	$ 7,211	$5,048
Mr. M. White	$12,255	$8,712

24. According to the information given above, which patient,
when compared with the other three patients, had the
HIGHEST percentage of his bill paid by the Insurance Plan?
  A. Mr. W. Smith   B. Mr. D. Harris
  C. Mr. T. Jones   D. Mr. M. White

25. The average amount paid by the Insurance Plan toward the   25.____
    hospital bills of the four patients shown above is MOST
    NEARLY
       A. $5,269   B. $5,499   C. $5,749   D. $5,766

_____

KEY (CORRECT ANSWERS)

1. D	11. D
2. C	12. C
3. A	13. B
4. B	14. D
5. D	15. D
6. B	16. A
7. A	17. A
8. B	18. C
9. C	19. B
10. A	20. C

21. C
22. A
23. D
24. A
25. C

_____

TEST 2

Questions 1-2.

DIRECTIONS: Questions 1 and 2 are to be answered on the basis of the information contained in the chart below.

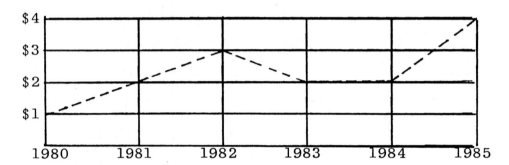

1. According to the above chart, the increase in the average   1
    price of the commodity from 1982 to 1985 was APPROXIMATELY
    A. 25%   B. 33 1/3%   C. 50%   D. 75%

2. According to the above chart, the increase in the average   2
    price of the commodity from 1980 to 1982 was APPROXIMATELY
    A. 20%   B. 30%   C. 200%   D. 300%

Questions 3-4.

DIRECTIONS: Questions 3 and 4 are to be answered SOLELY on the bas
of the information contained in the chart below, which shows supply and demand of a commodity from January 1, 1981 to January 1, 1985.

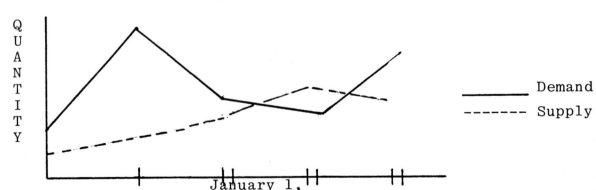

3. The above chart indicates that there was a seller's   3.___
   market during most of each of the following years EXCEPT
      A. 1981   B. 1982   C. 1983   D. 1984

4. According to the above chart, in the absence of price   4.___
   controls or other artificial or unusual circumstances,
   when would the price of the commodity have been the
   HIGHEST?
   January 1,
      A. 1981   B. 1982   C. 1983   D. 1984

5. In order to pay its employees, the Convex Company obtained   5.___
   bills and coins in the following denominations:

Denomination	$20	$10	$5	$1	$.50	$.25	$.10	$.05	$.01
Number	317	122	38	73	69	47	39	25	36

   What was the TOTAL amount of cash obtained?
      A. $7,874.76   B. $7,878.00
      C. $7,889.25   D. $7,924.35

6. Suppose that a business you are investigating presents the   6.___
   following figures:

Year	Net Income	Tax Rate On Net Income
1984	$55,000	20%
1985	$55,000	30%
1986	$65,000	20%
1987	$52,000	25%
1988	$62,000	30%
1989	$68,000	25%

   According to these figures, it is MOST accurate to say that
      A. less tax was due in 1988 than in 1989
      B. more tax was due in 1984 than in 1987
      C. the same amount of tax was due in 1984 and 1985
      D. the same amount of tax was due in 1986 and 1987

7. The table below shows the total amount of money owed on   7.___
   the bills sent to each of four different accounts and
   the total amount of money which has been received from
   each of these accounts.

Name of Account	Amount Owed	Amount Received
Arnold	$55,989	$37,898
Barry	$97,276	$79,457
Carter	$62,736	$47,769
Daley	$77,463	$59,534

   The balance of an account is determined by subtracting
   the amount received from the amount owed.
   Based on this method of determining a balance, the account
   with the LARGEST balance is
      A. Arnold   B. Barry   C. Carter   D. Daley

8. A work sheet for a booth audit has the readings shown   8
    below for four turnstiles:

Turnstile No.	Opening Readings	Readings For Audit
1	26178	26291
2	65489	65752
3	72267	72312
4	45965	46199

    With a fare of $1.00, what is the cash value of the TOTAL
    difference between the Opening Readings and the Readings
    for Audit for the four turnstiles?
    A. $635   B. $653   C. $654   D. $675

Questions 9-10.

DIRECTIONS: Questions 9 and 10 are to be answered SOLELY on the ba
               of the information contained in the following table.

COMPARISON OF CUNY ATTRITION RATES FOR FALL 1980 DAY FRESHMEN
                THROUGH FALL 1981

Colleges	Open Admissions (a)	Regular (b)	Overall
Senior	30%	14%	21%
Community	40%	34%	39%
Total	36%	20%	29%

(a) Represents senior college students admitted with high school
    averages below 80 and community college students admitted
    with high school averages below 75
(b) Represents senior college students admitted with averages of
    80 and above and community college students admitted with
    averages of 75 and above

9. The category of students who remained in the City   9
    University in the GREATEST proportion were
        A. regular students in community colleges
        B. open admissions students in community colleges
        C. regular students in senior colleges
        D. open admissions students in senior colleges

10. Regular admission to a senior college was on the basis of   10
    an academic average
        A. above 70   B. of 80 or above
        C. above 75   D. above 85

Questions 11-12.

DIRECTIONS: Questions 11 and 12 are to be answered SOLELY on the basis of the information given below.

Time Scores

Maximum qualifying time	15 minutes
Minimum qualifying time (subtract)	5 minutes
Range in qualifying time	10 minutes

Weighted Point Scores (Weight = 10)

Maximum weighted score	10 points
Minimum qualifying score (subtract)	7 points
Range in weighted scores	3 points

From the foregoing, it is apparent that a simple conversion table can be prepared by giving the maximum qualifying time a minimum qualifying weighted score of 7 points and crediting three-tenths additional weighted points for each minute less than 15.

11. On the basis of the above paragraph, it is apparent that if the maximum *time* taken by any candidate on the task was 15 minutes,　　　　　　　　　　　　　　　　11.___
    A. the test was too easy
    B. too much weight was given to the *time* portion
    C. less time should have been given for the task
    D. no one failed the *time* portion of the test

12. The BEST of the following interpretations of the above paragraph is that any candidate completing the task in 8 minutes would have received a weighted score for *time* of ___ points.　　　　　　　　　　　　　　12.___
    　　A. 9.1　　　　　　B. 8.5　　　　　　C. 8.2　　　　　　D. 7.9

Questions 13-14.

DIRECTIONS: Questions 13 and 14 are to be answered on the basis of
the following illustration. Assume that the figures
in the chart are cubes.

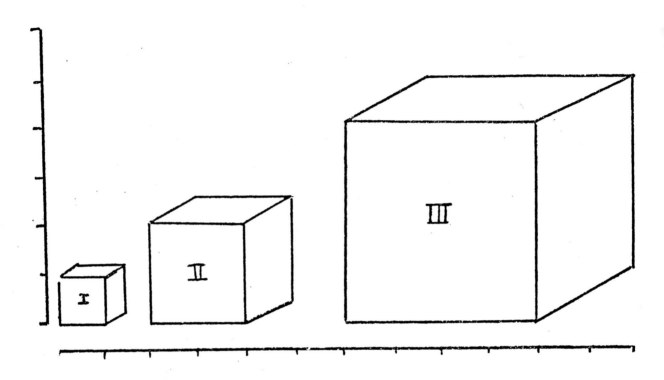

13.   In the illustration above, how many times GREATER is the   13
quantity represented by Figure III than the quantity
represented by Figure II?
   A. 2   B. 4   C. 8   D. 16

14.   The illustration above illustrates a progression in   14
quantity BEST described as
   A. arithmetic   B. geometric
   C. discrete   D. linear

Questions 15-16.

DIRECTIONS: Questions 15 and 16 are to be answered SOLELY on the
basis of the following summary of salary increases
applicable to a group of employees in a college office

Hourly Rate 6/30/82	Increase 7/1/82	Increase 7/1/83
$5.10	$.70/hr.	$.70/hr.
$5.60	$.60/hr.	$.60/hr.
$6.10	$.60/hr.	$.60/hr.

Hourly Rate 6/30/82	Increase 7/1/82	Increase 7/1/83
$6.60	$.50/hr.	$.50/hr.
$7.10	$.50/hr.	$.50/hr.
$7.60	$.50/hr.	$.50/hr.

15. A college office employee with an hourly salary of $7.10 15.___
    as of June 30, 1982 worked for 32 hours during the week
    of April 16, 1983.
    Her GROSS salary for that week was
       A. $211.20   B. $227.20   C. $243.20   D. $259.20

16. A college office employee was earning an hourly salary of 16.___
    $6.10 in June of 1982.
    The percentage increase in her hourly salary as of July 2,
    1983 will be MOST NEARLY _____ percent.
       A. 10   B. 15   C. 20   D. 25

17. An experiment was conducted to measure the error rate of 17.___
    typists. The results follow:

Typists	Percent of Total Output	Error Rate (in percent)
A	30	1.00
B	30	1.50
C	40	0.50

The error rate (in percent) for the three typists combined
   A. is 0.95
   B. is 1.00
   C. is 3.00
   D. cannot be calculated from the given data

Question 18.

DIRECTIONS: Question 18 is to be answered on the basis of the
             information given below.

At midnight on January 31, the following bodies were
remaining:

Adults	Infants	Stillbirths	Amputations
37	23	40	21

On February 1st, from 12:01 A.M. to 12:00 midnight, the
following bodies were received:

Adults	Infants	Stillbirths	Amputations
24	13	18	8

In addition, the following bodies were claimed:

Adults	Infants	Stillbirths	Amputations
33	9	4	2

18. What is the number of cases remaining at midnight on   18
    February 1?

	Adults	Infants	Stillbirths	Amputations
A.	31	26	41	23
B.	28	27	54	27
C.	29	28	48	25
D.	27	29	62	28

Questions 19-25.

DIRECTIONS: Questions 19 through 25 are to be answered SOLELY on
               the basis of the following information.

<u>ACCIDENTS</u>

During one month, a certain division reported the number of
accidents from various causes as follows:

        Falls 6
        Flying objects............ 5
        Handling objects.......... 4
        Striking objects.......... 3
        Assaults.................. 2
        Stepping on objects....... 1

19. The GREATEST cause of accidents was   19
    A. striking objects   B. handling objects
    C. flying objects   D. falls

20. The accidents over which the injured person had LEAST   20
    control were those due to
    A. handling objects   B. falls
    C. assaults   D. flying objects

21. The accidents due to flying objects exceeded those due to   21
    striking objects by
    A. 8   B. 6   C. 3   D. 2

22. The TOTAL number of accidents as shown was   22
    A. 19   B. 20   C. 21   D. 22

23. The MOST likely cause for an accident to a station porter   23
    is
    A. stepping on objects   B. falls
    C. striking objects   D. assaults

24. The accidents which would MOST likely result in disciplin- 24
    ary action are those due to
    A. stepping on objects   B. assaults
    C. striking objects   D. falls

25. The TOTAL number of accidents involving objects was   25
    A. 8   B. 12   C. 13   D. 21

KEY (CORRECT ANSWERS)

1.	B	11.	D
2.	C	12.	A
3.	C	13.	C
4.	B	14.	B
5.	A	15.	C
6.	D	16.	C
7.	A	17.	A
8.	C	18.	B
9.	C	19.	D
10.	B	20.	D

21. D
22. C
23. B
24. B
25. C

ARITHMETICAL REASONING
EXAMINATION SECTION
TEST 1

DIRECTIONS: Each question or incomplete statement is followed by several suggested answers or completions. Select the one that BEST answers the question or completes the statement. *PRINT THE LETTER OF THE CORRECT ANSWER IN THE SPACE AT THE RIGHT.*

1. The ABC Corporation had a gross income of $125,500.00 in 2004. Of this, it paid 60% for overhead.
   If the gross income for 2005 increased by $6,500 and the cost of overhead increased to 61% of gross income, how much MORE did it pay for overhead in 2005 than in 2004?
   A. $1,320   B. $5,220   C. $7,530   D. $8,052   1.___

2. After one year, Mr. Richards paid back a total of $16,950 as payment for a $15,000 loan. All the money paid over $15,000 was simple interest.
   The interest charge was MOST NEARLY
   A. 13%   B. 11%   C. 9%   D. 7%   2.___

3. A checking account has a balance of $253.36.
   If deposits of $36.95, $210.23, and $7.34 and withdrawals of $117.35, $23.37, and $15.98 are made, what is the NEW balance of the account?
   A. $155.54   B. $351.18   C. $364.58   D. $664.58   3.___

4. In 2004, The W Realty Company spent 27% of its income on rent.
   If it earned $97,254 in 2004, the amount it paid for rent was
   A. $26,258.58   B. $26,348.58
   C. $27,248.58   D. $27,358.58   4.___

5. Six percent simple annual interest on $2,436.18 is MOST NEARLY
   A. $145.08   B. $145.17   C. $146.08   D. $146.17   5.___

6. H. Partridge receives a weekly gross salary (before deductions) of $397.50. Through weekly payroll deductions of $13.18, he is paying back a loan he took from his pension fund.
   If other fixed weekly deductions amount to $122.76, how much pay would Mr. Partridge take home over a period of 33 weeks?
   A. $7,631.28   B. $8,250.46   C. $8,631.48   D. $13,117.50   6.___

7. Mr. Robertson is a city employee enrolled in a city retirement system. He has taken out a loan from the retirement fund and is paying it back at the rate of $14.90 every two weeks.
   In eighteen weeks, how much money will he have paid back on the loan?
   A. $268.20   B. $152.80   C. $134.10   D. $67.05   7.___

8. In 2004, The Iridor Book Company had the following   8.__
   expenses: rent, $6,500; overhead, $52,585; inventory,
   $35,700; and miscellaneous, $1,275.
   If all of these expenses went up 18% in 2005, what
   would they TOTAL in 2005?
      A. $17,290.80   B. $78,769.20
      C. $96,060.00   D. $113,350.80

9. Ms. Ranier had a gross salary of $710.72 paid once every   9.__
   two weeks.
   If the deductions from each paycheck are $125.44, $50.26,
   $12.58, and $2.54, how much money would Ms. Ranier take
   home in eight weeks?
      A. $2,079.60 B. $2,842.88 C. $4,159.20 D. $5,685.76

10. Mr. Martin had a net income of $95,500 in 2004.   10.__
    If he spent 34% on rent and household expenses, 3% on
    house furnishings, 25% on clothes, and 36% on food, how
    much was left for savings and other expenses?
       A. $980   B. $1,910   C. $3,247   D. $9,800

11. Mr. Elsberg can pay back a loan of $1,800 from the city   11.__
    employees' retirement system if he pays back $36.69
    every two weeks for two full years.
    At the end of the two years, how much more than the
    original $1,800 he borrowed will Mr. Elsberg have paid
    back?
       A. $53.94   B. $107.88   C. $190.79   D. $214.76

12. Mr. Nusbaum is a city employee receiving a gross salary   12.__
    (salary before deductions) of $20,800. Every two weeks
    the following deductions are taken out of his salary:
    Federal Income Tax, $162.84; FICA, $44.26; State Tax,
    $29.72; City Tax, $13.94; Health Insurance, $3.14.
    If Mr. Nusbaum's salary and deductions remained the same
    for a full calendar year, what would his net salary
    (gross salary less deductions) be in that year?
       A. $6,596.20   B. $14,198.60
       C. $18,745.50   D. $20,546.30

13. Add: 8936   13.__
           7821
           8953
           4297
           9785
           6579

       A. 45,371   B. 45,381   C. 46,371   D. 46,381

14. Multiply: 987   14.__
               867

       A. 854,609   B. 854,729   C. 855,709   D. 855,729

15. Divide: 59)$\overline{321439.0}$ 15.___

    A. 5438.1   B. 5447.1   C. 5448.1   D. 5457.1

16. Divide: .057)$\overline{721}$ 16.___

    A. 12,648.0   B. 12,648.1   C. 12,649.0   D. 12,649.1

17. If the total number of employees in one city agency   17.___
    increased from 1,927 to 2,006 during a certain year,
    the percentage increase in the number of employees for
    that year is MOST NEARLY
    A. 4%   B. 5%   C. 6%   D. 7%

18. During a single fiscal year, which totaled 248 workdays,   18.___
    one account clerk verified 1,488 purchase vouchers.
    Assuming a normal work week of five days, what is the
    AVERAGE number of vouchers verified by the account clerk
    in a one-week period during this fiscal year?
    A. 25   B. 30   C. 35   D. 40

19. Multiplying a number by .75 is the same as   19.___
    A. multiplying it by 2/3   B. dividing it by 2/3
    C. multiplying it by 3/4   D. dividing it by 3/4

20. In City Agency A, 2/3 of the employees are enrolled in   20.___
    a retirement system. City Agency B has the same number
    of employees as Agency A, and 60% of these are enrolled
    in a retirement system.
    If Agency A has a total of 660 employees, how many MORE
    employees does it have enrolled in a retirement system
    than does Agency B?
    A. 36   B. 44   C. 56   D. 66

21. Net worth is equal to assets minus liabilities.   21.___
    If, at the end of 2003, a textile company had assets of
    $98,695.83 and liabilities of $59,238.29, what was its
    net worth?
    A. $38,478.54   B. $38,488.64
    C. $39,457.54   D. $48,557.54

22. Mr. Martin's assets consist of the following: 22.___
        Cash on hand $ 5,233.74
        Automobile   3,206.09
        Furniture   4,925.00
        Government Bonds   5,500.00
        House   36,690.85
    What are his TOTAL assets?
    A. $54,545.68   B. $54,455.68
    C. $55,455.68   D. $55,555.68

23. If Mr. Mitchell has $627.04 in his checking account and
    then writes three checks for $241.75, $13.24, and $102.97,
    what will be his new balance?
    A. $257.88   B. $269.08   C. $357.96   D. $369.96

23. _

24. An employee's net pay is equal to his total earnings less
    all deductions.
    If an employee's total earnings in a pay period are
    $497.05, what is his net pay if he has the following
    deductions: Federal income tax, $90.32; FICA, $28.74;
    State tax, $18.79; City tax, $7.25; Pension, $1.88?
    A. $351.17   B. $351.07   C. $350.17   D. $350.07

24. _

25. A petty cash fund had an opening balance of $85.75 on
    December 1. Expenditures of $23.00, $15.65, $5.23,
    $14.75, and $26.38 were made out of this fund during
    the first 14 days of the month. Then, on December 17,
    another $38.50 was added to the fund.
    If additional expenditures of $17.18, $3.29, and $11.64
    were made during the remainder of the month, what was
    the FINAL balance of the petty cash fund at the end of
    December?
    A. $6.93   B. $7.13   C. $46.51   D. $91.40

25. _

———

KEY (CORRECT ANSWERS)

1. B	11. B
2. A	12. B
3. B	13. C
4. A	14. D
5. D	15. C
6. C	16. D
7. C	17. A
8. D	18. B
9. A	19. C
10. B	20. B

21. C
22. D
23. B
24. D
25. B

———

SOLUTIONS TO PROBLEMS

1. ($132,000)(.61)-($125,500)(.60) = $5220

2. Interest = $1950. As a percent, $1950 ÷ 15,000 = 13%

3. New balance = $253.36 + $36.95 + $210.23 + $7.34 - $117.35 - $23.37 - $15.98 = $351.18

4. Rent = ($97,254)(.27) = $26,258.58

5. ($2436.18)(.06) ≈ $146.17

6. ($397.50-$13.18-$122.76)(33) = $8631.48

7. ($14.90)($\frac{18}{2}$) = $134.10

8. ($6500+$52,585+$35,700+$1275)(1.18) = $113,350.80

9. ($710.72-$125.44-$50.26-$12.58-$2.54)($\frac{8}{2}$) = $2079.60

10. (1-.34-.03-.25-.36)($95,500) = $1910

11. ($36.69)(52) - $1800 = $107.88

12. $20,800 - (26)($162.84+$44.26+$29.72+$13.94+$3.14) = $14,198.60

13. 8936 + 7821 + 8953 + 4297 + 9785 + 6579 = 46,371

14. (987)(867) = 855,729

15. 321,439 ÷ 59 ≈ 5448.1

16. 721 ÷ .057 ≈ 12,649.1

17. (2006-1927) ÷ 1927 ≈ 4%

18. Let x = number of vouchers. Then, $\frac{x}{5} = \frac{1488}{248}$. Solving, x = 30

19. Multiplying by .75 is equivalent to multiplying by $\frac{3}{4}$

20. (660)($\frac{2}{3}$) - (660)(.60) = 44

21. Net worth = $98,695.83 - $59,238.29 = $39,457.54

22. Total assets = $5233.74 + $3206.09 + $4925.00 + $5500.00 + $36,690.85 = $55,555.68

23. New balance = $627.04 - $241.75 - $13.24 - $102.97 = $269.08

24. Net pay = $497.05 - $90.32 - $28.74 - $18.79 - $7.25 - $1.88
    = $350.07

25. Final balance = $85.75 - $23.00 - $15.65 - $5.23 - $14.75 -
    $26.38 + $38.50 - $17.18 - $3.29 - $11.64 = $7.13

TEST 2

DIRECTIONS: Each question or incomplete statement is followed by several suggested answers or completions. Select the one that BEST answers the question or completes the statement. *PRINT THE LETTER OF THE CORRECT ANSWER IN THE SPACE AT THE RIGHT.*

1. The formula for computing base salary is: Earnings equals base gross plus additional gross.
   If an employee's earnings during a particular period are in the amounts of $597.45, $535.92, $639.91, and $552.83, and his base gross salary is $525.50 per paycheck, what is the TOTAL of the additional gross earned by the employee during that period?
   A. $224.11   B. $224.21   C. $224.51   D. $244.11   1.____

2. If a lump sum death benefit is paid by the retirement system in an amount equal to 3/7 of an employee's last yearly salary of $13,486.50, the amount of the death benefit paid is MOST NEARLY
   A. $5,749.29 B. $5,759.92 C. $5,779.92 D. $5,977.29   2.____

3. Suppose that a member has paid 15 installments on a 28-installment loan.
   The percentage of the number of installments paid to the retirement system is
   A. 53.57%   B. 53.97%   C. 54.57%   D. 55.37%   3.____

4. If an employee takes a 1-month vacation during a calendar year, the percentage of the year during which he works is MOST NEARLY
   A. 90.9%   B. 91.3%   C. 91.6%   D. 92.1%   4.____

5. Suppose that an employee took a leave of absence totaling 7 months during a calendar year.
   Assuming the employee did not take any vacation time during the remainder of that year, the percentage of the year in which he worked is MOST NEARLY
   A. 41.7%   B. 43.3%   C. 46.5%   D. 47.1%   5.____

6. A member has borrowed $4,725 from her funds in the retirement system.
   If $3,213 has been repaid, the percentage of the loan which is still outstanding is MOST NEARLY
   A. 16%   B. 32%   C. 48%   D. 68%   6.____

7. If an employee worked only 24 weeks during the year because of illness, the portion of the year he was out of work was MOST NEARLY
   A. 46%   B. 48%   C. 51%   D. 54%   7.____

8. If an employee purchased credit for a 16-week period of   8.__
   service which he had prior to rejoining the retirement
   system, the percentage of a year he purchased credit
   for was MOST NEARLY
       A. 27.9%   B. 28.8%   C. 30.7%   D. 33.3%

9. If an employee contributes 2/11 of his yearly salary to   9.__
   his pension fund account, the percentage of his yearly
   salary which he contributes is MOST NEARLY
       A. 17.9%   B. 18.2%   C. 18.4%   D. 19.0%

10. In 1975, the maximum amount of income from which social   10.__
    security tax could be withheld (base salary) was $14,100.
    In 1977, the base salary was $16,500.
    The 1977 base salary represents a percentage increase
    over the 1975 base salary of approximately
       A. 15%   B. 16%   C. 17%   D. 18%

11. If 17.5% of an employee's salary is withheld for taxes,   11.__
    the one of the following which is the fraction of the
    salary withheld is
       A. 3/20   B. 8/35   C. 7/40   D. 4/25

12. If a person withdraws 42% of the funds from his account   12.__
    with the retirement system, the remaining balance repre-
    sents a fraction of MOST NEARLY
       A. 7/13   B. 5/9   C. 7/12   D. 4/7

13. A property decreases in value from $45,000 to $35,000.   13.__
    The percent of decrease is MOST NEARLY
       A. 20.5%   B. 22.2%   C. 25.0%   D. 28.6%

14. The fraction $\frac{487}{101326}$ expressed as a decimal is MOST NEARLY   14.__

       A. .0482   B. .00481   C. .0049   D. .00392

15. The reciprocal of the sum of 2/3 and 1/6 can be expressed 15.__
    as
       A. 0.83   B. 1.20   C. 1.25   D. 1.50

16. Total land and building costs for a new commercial proper- 16.__
    ty equal $50 per square foot.
    If the investors expect a 10 percent return on their
    costs, and if total operating expenses average 5 percent
    of total costs, annual gross rentals per square foot must
    be AT LEAST
       A. $7.50   B. $8.50   C. $10.00   D. $12.00

17. The formula for computing the amount of annual deposit in 17.__
    a compound interest bearing account to provide a lump sum

    at the end of a period of years is $X = \frac{r.L}{(1+r)^{n}-1}$ (X is the

    amount of annual deposit, r is the rate of interest, and
    n is the number of years) and L = lump sum)

Using the formula, the annual amount of the deposit at
the end of each year to accumulate to $20,000 at the end
of 3 years with interest at 2 percent on annual balances
is
  A. $6,120.00 B. $6,203.33 C. $6,535.09 D. $6,666.66

18. An investor sold two properties at $150,000 each. On one   18.___
    he made a 25 percent profit. On the other he suffered a
    25 percent loss.
    The NET result of his sales was
      A. neither a gain nor a loss
      B. a $20,000 loss
      C. a $75,000 gain
      D. a $75,000 loss

19. A contractor decides to install a chain fence covering   19.___
    the perimeter of a parcel 75 feet wide and 112 feet in
    depth.
    Which one of the following represents the number of feet
    to be covered?
      A. 187   B. 364   C. 374   D. 8,400

20. A builder estimates he can build an average of $4\frac{1}{2}$ one-   20.___
    family homes to an acre. There are 640 acres to one
    square mile.
    Which one of the following CORRECTLY represents the
    number of one-family homes the builder would estimate he
    can build on one square mile?
      A. 1,280   B. 1,920   C. 2,560   D. 2,880

21. $.01059 deposited at 7 percent interest will yield $1.00   21.___
    in 30 years.
    If a person deposited $1,059 at 7 percent interest on
    April 1, 1974, which one of the following amounts would
    represent the worth of this deposit on March 31, 2004?
      A. $100   B. $1,000   C. $10,000   D. $100,000

22. A building has an economic life of forty years.   22.___
    Assuming the building depreciates at a constant annual
    rate, which one of the following CORRECTLY represents
    the yearly percentage of depreciation?
      A. 2.0%   B. 2.5%   C. 5.0%   D. 7.0%

23. A building produces a gross income of $200,000 with a   23.___
    net income of $20,000, before mortgage charges and capital
    recapture. The owner is able to increase the gross
    income 5 percent without a corresponding increase in
    operating costs.
    The effect upon the net income will be an INCREASE of
      A. 5%   B. 10%   C. 12.5%   D. 50%

24. The present value of $1.00 not payable for 8 years, and   24.__
    at 10 percent interest, is $.4665.
    Which of the following amounts represents the PRESENT
    value of $1,000 payable 8 years hence at 10 percent
    interest?
       A. $46.65   B. $466.50   C. $4,665.00 D. $46,650.00

25. The amount of real property taxes to be levied by a city   25.__
    is $100 million. The assessment roll subject to taxation
    shows an assessed valuation of $2 billion.
    Which one of the following tax rates CORRECTLY represents
    the tax rate to be levied per $100 of assessed valuation?
       A. $.50   B. $5.00   C. $50.00   D. $500.00

———

KEY (CORRECT ANSWERS)

1. A		11. C	
2. C		12. C	
3. A		13. B	
4. C		14. B	
5. A		15. B	
6. B		16. A	
7. D		17. C	
8. C		18. B	
9. B		19. C	
10. C		20. D	

21. D
22. B
23. D
24. B
25. B

———

SOLUTIONS TO PROBLEMS

1. $597.45 + $535.92 + $639.91 + $552.83 = $2326.11
    Then, $2326.11 - (4)($525.50) = $224.11

2. Death benefit = ($13,486.50)$(\frac{3}{7})$ ≈ $5779.92

3. $\frac{15}{28}$ ≈ 53.57%

4. $\frac{11}{12}$ ≈ 91.6% (closer to 91.7%)

5. $\frac{5}{12}$ ≈ 41.7%

6. ($4725-$3213) ÷ $4725 = 32%

7. $\frac{28}{52}$ ≈ 54%

8. $\frac{16}{52}$ ≈ 30.7% (closer to 30.8%)

9. $\frac{2}{11}$ ≈ 18.2%

10. ($16,500-$14,100) ÷ $14,100 ≈ 17%

11. 17.5% = $\frac{175}{1000}$ = $\frac{7}{40}$

12. 100% - 42% = 58% = $\frac{58}{100}$ = $\frac{29}{50}$, closest to $\frac{7}{12}$ in selections

13. $\frac{$10,000}{$45,000}$ ≈ 22.2%

14. 487/101,326 ≈ .00481

15. $\frac{2}{3}$ + $\frac{1}{6}$ = $\frac{5}{6}$ Then, 1 ÷ $\frac{5}{6}$ = $\frac{6}{5}$ = 1.20

16. (.15)($50) = $7.50

17. x = (.02)($20,000)/[(1+.02)^3-1] = 400 ÷ .061208 ≈ $6535.09

18. Sold 150,000, 25% loss = paid 200,000, loss of 50,000
    Sold 150,000, 25% profit = paid 120,000, profit of 30,000
    - 50,000 + 30,000 = -20,000 (loss)

19. Perimeter = (2)(75')+(2)(112') = 374 ft.

20. (640)(4$\frac{1}{2}$) = 2880 homes

21. $(1 \div .01059)(1059) = \$100,000$

22. $1 \div 40 = .025 = 2.5\%$

23. New gross income $= (\$200,000)(1.05) = \$210,000.$
    Then, $(\$210,000 - \$200,000) \div \$20,000 = 50\%$

24. Let x = present value of $1000. Then, $\dfrac{\$1.00}{\$.4665} = \dfrac{\$1000}{x}$

    Solving, $x = \$466.50$

25. Let x = tax rate. Then, $\dfrac{\$100,000,000}{\$2,000,000,000} = \dfrac{x}{\$100}$

    Solving, $x = \$5.00$

TEST 3

1. It is found that for the past three years the average weekly number of inspections per inspector ranged from 20 inspections to 40 inspections.
   On the basis of this information, it is MOST reasonable to conclude that
   A. on the average, 30 inspections per week were made
   B. the average weekly number of inspections never fell below 20
   C. the performance of inspectors deteriorated over the three-year period
   D. the range in average weekly inspections was 60

1.___

Questions 2-4.

DIRECTIONS: Questions 2 through 4 are to be answered on the basis of the following information.

The number of students admitted to University X in 2004 from High School Y was 268 students. This represented 13.7 percent of University X's entering freshman classes. In 2005, it is expected that University X will admit 591 students from High School Y, which is expected to represent 19.4 percent of the 2005 entering freshman classes of University X.

2. Which of the following is the CLOSEST estimate of the size of University X's expected 2005 entering freshman classes?
   _____ students.
   A. 2,000   B. 2,500   C. 3,000   D. 3,500

2.___

3. Of the following, the expected percentage of increase from 2004 to 2005 in the number of students graduating from High School Y and entering University X as freshmen is MOST NEARLY
   A. 5.7%   B. 20%   C. 45%   D. 120%

3.___

4. Assume that the cost of processing each freshman admission to University X from High School Y in 2004 was an average of $28. Also, that this was 1/3 more than the average cost of processing each of the other 2004 freshman admissions to University X.
   Then, the one of the following that MOST closely shows the total processing cost of all 2004 freshman admissions to University X is
   A. $6,500   B. $20,000   C. $30,000   D. $40,000

4.___

5. Assume that during the fiscal year 2005-2006, a bureau
produced 20% more work units than it produced in the
fiscal year 2004-2005. Also assume that during the
fiscal year 2005-2006 that bureau's staff was 20% smaller
than it was in the fiscal year 2004-2005.
On the basis of this information, it would be MOST proper
to conclude that the number of work units produced per
staff member in that bureau in the fiscal year 2005-2006
exceeded the number of work units produced per staff
member in that bureau in the fiscal year 2004-2005 by
which one of the following percentages?
   A. 20%   B. 25%   C. 40%   D. 50%

6. Assume that during the following five fiscal years (FY),
a bureau has received the following appropriations:
   FY 2002-2003 - $200,000
   FY 2003-2004 - $240,000
   FY 2004-2005 - $280,000
   FY 2005-2006 - $390,000
   FY 2006-2007 - $505,000
The bureau's appropriation for which one of the following
fiscal years showed the LARGEST percentage of increase
over the bureau's appropriation for the immediately
previous fiscal year?
   A. FY 2003-2004   B. FY 2004-2005
   C. FY 2005-2006   D. FY 2006-2007

7. Assume that the number of buses (U_t) required for a given
line-haul system serving the Central Business District
depends upon roundtrip time (t), capacity of bus (c), and
the total number of people to be moved in a peak hour (P)
in the major direction, i.e., in the morning and out in
the evening.
The formula for the number of buses required is

   A. $U_t = Ptc$ B. $U_t = \frac{tP}{c}$ C. $U_t = \frac{cP}{t}$ D. $U_t = \frac{ct}{P}$

8. The area, in blocks, that can be served by a single stop
for any maximum walking distance is given by the following
formula: $a = 2w^2$. In this formula, a = the area served
by a stop, and w = maximum walking distance.
If people will tolerate a walk of up to three blocks, how
many stops would be needed to service an area of 288
square blocks?
   A. 9   B. 16   C. 18   D. 27

Questions 9-11.

DIRECTIONS: Questions 9 through 11 are to be answered on the basis
            of the following information.

    In 2006, a police precinct records 456 cases of car thefts which
is 22.6 percent of all grand larcenies. In 2007, there were 560 such
cases, which constituted 35% of the broader category.

9. The number of crimes in the broader category in 2007 was 9.___
MOST NEARLY
   A. 1,600   B. 1,700   C. 1,960   D. 2,800

10. The change from 2006 to 2007 in the number of crimes in 10.___
the broader category represented MOST NEARLY a
   A. 2.5% decrease   B. 10.1% increase
   C. 12.5% increase   D. 20% decrease

11. In 2007, one out of every 6 of these crimes was solved. 11.___
This represents MOST NEARLY what percentage of the total
number of crimes in the broader category that year?
   A. 5.8   B. 6   C. 9.3   D. 12

12. Assume that a maintenance shop does 5 brake jobs to every 12.___
3 front-end jobs. It does 8,000 jobs altogether in a
240-day year. In one day, one worker can do 3 front-end
jobs or 4 brake jobs.
About how many workers will be needed in the shop?
   A. 3   B. 5   C. 10   D. 18

13. Assume that the price of a certain item declines by 6% 13.___
one year, and then increases by 5 and 10 percent, respectively, during the next two years.
What is the OVERALL increase in price over the three-year
period?
   A. 4.2   B. 6   C. 8.6   D. 10.1

14. After finding the total percent change in a price (TC) 14.___
over a three-year period, as in the preceding question,
one could compute the average annual percent change in
the price by using the formula

   A. $(1 + TC)^{1/3}$ B. $\dfrac{(1 + TC)}{3}$

   C. $(1 + TC)^{1/3} - 1$ D. $\dfrac{1}{(1 + TC)^{1/3} - 1}$

15. 357 is 6% of 15.___
   A. 2,142   B. 5,950   C. 4,140   D. 5,900

16. In 2002, a department bought n pieces of a certain supply 16.___
item for a total of $x. In 2003, the department bought
k percent fewer of the item but had to pay a total of g
percent more for it.
Which of the following formulas is CORRECT for determining
the average price per item in 2003?

   A. $100 \dfrac{xg}{nk}$ B. $\dfrac{x(100 + g)}{n(100 - k)}$

   C. $\dfrac{x(100 - g)}{n(100 + k)}$ D. $\dfrac{x}{n} - 100 \dfrac{g}{k}$

17. A sample of 18 income tax returns, each with 4 personal exemptions, is taken for 2001 and for 2002. The break-down is as follows in terms of income:

Average gross income (in thousands)	Number of returns 2001	2002
40	6	2
80	10	11
120	2	5

There is a personal deduction per exemption of $500. There are no other expense deductions. In addition, there is an exclusion of $3,000 for incomes less than $50,000 and $2,000 for incomes from $50,000 to $99,999.99. From $100,000 upward there is no exclusion.
The average net taxable income for the samples in thousands) for 2001 is MOST NEARLY

    A. $67   B. $85   C. $10   D. $128

18. In the preceding question, the increase in average net taxable income for the sample (in thousands) between 2001 and 2002 is

    A. 16   B. 20   C. 24   D. 34

19. Assume that supervisor S has four subordinates - A, B, C, and D.
The MAXIMUM number of relationships, assuming that all combinations are included, that can exist between S and his subordinates is

    A. 28   B. 15   C. 7   D. 4

20. If the workmen's compensation insurance rate for clerical workers is 93 cents per $100 of wages, the total premium paid by a city whose clerical staff earns $8,765,000 is MOST NEARLY

    A. $8,150   B. $81,515   C. $87,650   D. $93,765

21. Assume that a budget of $3,240,000,000 for the fiscal year beginning July 1, 2003 has been approved. A city sales tax is expected to provide $1,100,000,000; licenses, fees and sundry revenues are expected to yield $121,600,000; the balance is to be raised from property taxes. A tax equalization board has appraised all property in the city at a fair value of $42,500,000,000. The council wishes to assess property at 60% of its fair value.
The tax rate would need to be MOST NEARLY _____ per $100 of assessed value.

    A. $12.70   B. $10.65   C. $7.90   D. $4.00

22. Men's white linen handkerchiefs cost $12.90 for 3. The cost per dozen handkerchiefs is

    A. $77.40   B. $38.70   C. $144.80   D. $51.60

23. Assume that it is necessary to partition a room measuring 40 feet by 20 feet into eight smaller rooms of equal size. Allowing no room for aisles, the MINIMUM amount of partitioning that would be needed is _____ feet.
    A. 90   B. 100   C. 110   D. 140

23.___

24. Assume that two types of files have been ordered: 200 of type A and 100 of type B. When the files are delivered, the buyer discovers that 25% of each type is damaged. Of the remaining files, 20% of type A and 40% of type B are the wrong color.
The total number of files that are the WRONG COLOR is
    A. 30   B. 40   C. 50   D. 60

24.___

25. In a unit of five inspectors, one inspector makes an average of 12 inspections a day, two inspectors make an average of 20 inspections a day, and two inspectors make an average of 9 inspections a day.
If in a certain week one of the inspectors who makes an average of nine inspections a day is out of work on Monday and Tuesday because of illness and all the inspectors do no inspections for half a day on Wednesday because of a special meeting, the number of inspections this unit can be expected to make in that week is MOST NEARLY
    A. 215   B. 225   C. 230   D. 250

25.___

KEY (CORRECT ANSWERS)

1. B		11. A	
2. C		12. C	
3. D		13. C	
4. D		14. C	
5. D		15. B	
6. C		16. B	
7. B		17. A	
8. B		18. A	
9. A		19. B	
10. D		20. B	

21. C
22. D
23. B
24. D
25. A

SOLUTIONS TO PROBLEMS

1. Since the number of weekly inspections ranged from 20 to 40, this implies that the average weekly number of inspections never fell below 20 (choice B).

2. $591 \div .194 \approx 3046$, closest to 3000 students

3. $(591-268) \div 268 \approx 120\%$

4. Total processing cost = $(268)(\$28)+(1688)(\$21) = \$42,952$, closest to \$40,000. [Note: Since 268 represents 13.7%, total freshman population = $268 \div .137 \approx 1956$. Then, $1956 - 268 = 1688$]

5. Let x = staff size in 2004-2005. Then, $.80x$ = staff size in 2005-2006. Since the 2005-2006 staff produced 20% more work, this is represented by 1.20. However, to measure the productivity per staff member, the factor $1/.80 = 1.25$ must also be used to equate the 2 staffs. Then, $(1.20)(1.25) = 1.50$. Thus, the 2005-2006 staff produced 50% more work than the 2004-2005 staff.

6. The respective percent increases are $\approx$ 20%, 17%, 39%, 29%. The largest would be, over the previous fiscal year, for the current fiscal year 2005-2006.

7. $\frac{P}{c}$ = number of buses needed per hour. If t = time (in hrs.), the $U_t = tP/c$

8. $a = (2)(9) = 18$ for 1 stop. Then, $288 \div 18 = 16$ stops

9. $560 \div .35 = 1600$ grand larcenies

10. $456 \div .226 \approx 2018$; $560 \div .35 = 1600$. Then, $(1600-2018) \div 2018 \approx -20\%$, or a 20% decrease

11. $(\frac{1}{6})(560) = 93\frac{1}{3}$. Then, $93\frac{1}{3} \div 1600 \approx 5.8\%$

12. There are 5000 brake jobs and 3000 front-end jobs in one year. $5000 \div 4 = 1250$ days, and $1250 \div 240 \approx 5.2$. Also, $3000 \div 3 = 1000$ days, and $1000 \div 240 \approx 4.2$. Total number of workers needed $\approx 5.2 + 4.2 \approx 10$

13. $(.94)(1.05)(1.10) = 1.0857$, which represents an overall increase by about 8.6%

14. Average annual % change = $(1+TC)^{\frac{1}{3}} - 1 = (1.0857)^{\frac{1}{3}} - 1 \approx 2.8\%$

15. $357 \div .06 = 5950$

16. In 2003, $(h)(1 - \frac{k}{100})$ pieces cost $(x)(1 + \frac{g}{100})$ dollars. To

calculate the cost for 1 piece (average cost), find the

value of $[(x)(1 + \frac{g}{100})] \div [(n)(1 - \frac{k}{100})] = [(x)(100+g)/100] \cdot$

$[100/\{n(100-k)\}] = [x(100+g)]/[n(100-k)]$

17.
	#	Deductions Up To 50,000		
40,000	6	2000	3000	40,000-3,000-2,000 = 35,000 × 6
80,000	10	2000	2000	80,000-2,000-2,000 = 75,000 × 10
120,000	2	2000		118000 × 2

35,000 × 6 = 210,000   = 210
76,000 × 10 = 760,000 = 760
118,000 × 2 = 236,000 = 236
                        1206

1206 ÷ 18 = 67

18.
2002		Deductions		
40,000	2	2000	3000	35,000 × 2 = 70,000
80,000	11	2000	2000	76,000 × 11 = 836,000
120,000	5	2000		118,000 × 5 = 590,000
				1496,000

1,496,000 ÷ 18 = 83,111
83,111 - 67,000 = 16,111 = most nearly 16 (in thousands)

19. We are actually looking for the number of different groups of
different sizes involving S. This reduces to $_4C_1 + {}_4C_2 + {}_4C_3 + {}_4C_4$ = 4 + 6 + 4 + 1 = 15. The notation $_nC_r$ means combinations
of n things taken R at a time = $[(n)(n-1)(n-2)(\ldots)(n-R+1)]/$
$[(R)(R-1)(\ldots)(1)]$. The 15 groups are: SA, SB, SC, SD, SAB,
SAC, SAD, SBC, SBD, SCD, SABC, SABD, SACD, SBCD, SABCD.

20. Let x = total premiums. Then, $\frac{.93}{100} = \frac{x}{8,765,000}$
Solving, x ≈ $81,515

21. The balance, raised from property taxes, = $3,240,000,000 -
$1,100,000,000 - $121,600,000 = $2,018,400,000. Now,
(.60)($42,500,000,000) = $25,500,000. The tax rate per $100
of assessed value = ($2,018,400,000)($100)/$25,500,000,000 ≈ $7.90

22. A dozen costs $(\$12.90)(\frac{12}{3})$ = $51.60

23. (40)(20) ÷ 8 = 100 ft.

24. Total number of wrong-color files = (200)(.75)(.20)+(100)(.75)(.40)
= 60

25. Total number of inspections = $(12)(4\frac{1}{2})+(20)(4\frac{1}{2})+(9)(2\frac{1}{2})+(4\frac{1}{2})(2)$
= 175.5   Closest entry is choice A.

GLOSSARY OF
LEGISLATIVE TERMS

CONTENTS

GLOSSARY OF
LEGISLATIVE TERMS

act, law, statute A legislative measure that has been passed by both houses of Congress and has been signed by the President, passed over his veto or allowed to become effective without his signature, i.e., a valid enactment. Although "act," "law" and "statute" are synonyms in this glossary, statute may also be defined as a formal written expression of the legislative will, thus distinguishing it from both unwritten and common (court made) law. *See also Law.*

adjournment *sine die* Literally, "adjournment without a day." Adjournment without naming a day for reconvening. Usually refers to the end of a session of Congress. Adjournment at the end of the second session terminates that Congress. Strictly speaking, Congress as such does not adjourn or convene; the separate houses do so. If the two disagree as to the time of adjournment, the President may adjourn them; but this power has never been used. Adjournment *sine die* is a fiction, of course, since the opening date of the next session is agreed upon by the leadership and is part of the motions to adjourn. *See also Congress and Session.*

administration bill (1) A legislative proposal transmitted in draft form by a Cabinet member, the head of an independent agency or the President to the House and Senate for introduction, usually by the chairpersons of the appropriate standing committees. The Constitution states that the President shall from time to time recommend to Congress the "consideration of such measures as he shall judge necessary and expedient." (2) A bill submitted by a leading member of the President's party and understood to have the strong support and approval of the Administration. Within recent years, many important measures have originated within the Executive Branch.

advance funding An appropriation providing funds for use in a fiscal year one or more years after the year for which the appropriation was enacted. Advance funding gives state and local governments an additional year in which to plan, with certainty, that funds will be available. Advance funding should be distinguished from "forward funding," which permits agencies to obligate (spend or commit) funds in the current fiscal year for programs that are to operate in subsequent fiscal years.

allocation Under certain federal grant-in-aid programs, the process of dividing appropriated funds equitably among the states (or other jurisdictions) in accordance with specified formulas based on such criteria as population, per capita income or the relative prevalence of the problems intended to be solved. Also, the process of further distributing state allotments among the ultimate recipients, such as school districts, within the states.

In many programs, each state is awarded a base amount plus additional funds alloted by formula. Receipt of funds may depend on the submission of an acceptable state plan detailing the further distribution of funds according to stated priorities. If a state or other unit fails to apply or does not qualify, its presumed allotment may be redistributed among the others. Both the state and federal levels may be allowed to retain a percentage of the appropriated funds for administration, and sometimes for discretionary awards not governed by the general formula. *See also Local Entitlement.*

amendment　(1) Subsequent legislation to alter, repeal or add to all or part of an existing law. An amendment in this sense is introduced as a bill, is acted upon in the usual way and signed by the President, as a public law. The revisions called for by amendments may range from technical or editorial changes to sweeping alterations in basic policy. The affected law may be reprinted as a compilation, *q.v.*, to incorporate such revisions.

(2) An amendment to a bill is language offered by a member, in committee or on the floor, to alter the effect of a proposed measure by changing or deleting matter, or to add provisions that may or may not be relevant. Amendments may be introduced at several points in the legislative process. *See also Germaneness; Rider.*

apportionment　The Constitution provides that Congress shall apportion membership in the House of Representatives according to a decennial census, with each state to have at least one representative. Following the Apportionment Act of 1941, the process has been almost automatic, requiring only the review of Congress. Apportionment has been readjusted in every decade since 1870, except after the census of 1920. In 1929, the total number of representatives was fixed by law at 435, with the result that growth in one group of states means a loss of numerical representation for others.

When a state has only one representative, election is necessarily "at large." In states with more than one representative, each must represent a separate district and at large representation is not allowed. After reapportionment, each state may redistrict internally according to its own election laws. Within each state, districts must be substantially equal in population. Currently, the typical district in any but the smaller states has a population of somewhat less than one-half million. *See also Congress, Composition of House and Senate.*

appropriation　An act of Congress that permits agencies to incur obligations and make payments out of the Federal Treasury for specified purposes, but not necessarily in the amounts indicated by the authorizing legislation. Appropriations are characterized by their period of availability (one-year, multiple-year, no-year); the timing of Congressional action (temporary or permanent); and the way in which the amounts are indicated (definite or indefinite).

While appropriations bills are almost always introduced in the House, they are referred to committee, debated, amended and voted on by both houses. The Constitution specifies that all revenue (tax) measures must be initiated by the House; as a matter of practice, this rule has been extended to include spending measures as well. General appropriations are supposed to be enacted prior to the fiscal year to which they apply. In actuality, this may fail to happen and a continuing resolution, *q.v.*, must be passed to keep the affected agencies in operation. *See also Authorization; Supplemental Appropriation.*

authorization　An act approving a project, program or activity, outlining its purposes and procedures, assigning authority for its administration and, usually, fixing maximum amounts to be expended upon it. Authorizing legislation may establish appropriations ceilings for specific fiscal years or, less frequently today, it may call for "such sums as Congress may deem necessary." Authorization is the first step in the expenditure of funds, appropriations being the next. *See also Appropriation; Full Funding.*

bicameral legislature

A legislature made up of two houses or chambers, e.g., the Senate and House of Representatives, which must concur in the passage of legislation. This structure, which was arrived at as one of the important compromises in the drafting of the Constitution, has been followed by all of the states, with the exception of Nebraska, which has had a unicameral (one-house) legislature since 1934.

bill

The draft of a proposed law from the time of its introduction in either house, through all of the various stages in both houses, until its approval by the President or passage over his veto, when it becomes a law. Most proposals in Congress take the form of bills. Public bills deal with matters of national importance and are intended to create general law. Private bills, *q.v.,* seek relief for individuals with regard to immigration and naturalization, claims against the United States, etc. *Compare Concurrent Resolutions, Joint Resolutions.*

bill drafting

A legislative proposal must be expressed in concise terms to carry out the intent of its sponsors, avoid conflict with existing laws and guard against annulment in the courts. Since 1918, each congressional house has had an Office of Legislative Counsel prepared to offer technical assistance to the members. Many organizations interested in legislative developments employ expert draftsmen to prepare specialized language for bills and amendments to be submitted by members. Thus, bill drafting may be part of the work of a lobbyist.

bill numbering

Bills are numbered in each house in the order of their introduction, from the beginning of each two-year Congress, and bear the designation of the house in which they originated, e.g., S. 63, H.R. 1639. Pending bills lapse at the end of the Congress. If they are re-introduced, they are numbered as new bills and enter the process from the beginning. When a bill is passed by one house and submitted to the other, it retains its number and is reprinted with a notation to the effect that it is "in the" House or Senate.

block grant

A financial grant from one level of government to another that allows complete or at least fairly wide discretion on the part of the recipient, whose use of the funds would be limited, at the outside, by nothing more than its own organic act or charter. *Compare Categorical Programs.*

budget

A balanced estimate of expenditures and revenues for a stated fiscal period, for the purpose of effectuating an orderly financial policy. Traditionally, the preparation of the budget is one of the prime responsibilities of the executive branch under a representative form of government.

categorical programs

Grant-in-aid programs designed to deal with specific problems, implement narrowly defined policies and priorities, or benefit certain classes of recipients. Awards are made upon review of applications or proposals, often unsolicited. Several hundred federal categorical programs are believed to exist, each with its own guidelines, regulations, reports, rules of eligibility and entrenched bureaucracy. The same pattern exists at the state level. *Compare Block Grants.*

clerk of the house Chief administrative officer of the House (not a member), with duties similar to those of the Secretary of the Senate. He is a continuing officer whose duties do not terminate upon adjournment *sine die*, and presides at the opening of the newly-convened House until a Speaker is elected. He attests bills, resolutions and subpoenas, is custodian of the Seal, prepares the roll of members-elect, supervises House personnel and generally takes care of the House-keeping.

cloture A parliamentary device for halting debate and bringing an issue to a vote, used in the Senate to end filibusters. A vote to invoke cloture must be taken within two days after a petition has been submitted by 16 senators. If three-fifths of the entire membership (60 if there are no vacancies) votes for cloture, each senator will be allowed up to one hour of debate on the pending bill; then the measure must be brought to a final vote. Successful cloture in the Senate is rare (between 1917 and 1976, only 28 out of 108 attempts were carried). In the House, termination of debate may be accomplished by a majority vote on the previous question—a usual way of bringing a bill to a vote.

committee Where most legislative work is done. A designated body of either house, empowered to examine and report on pending legislation, or conduct investigations and studies as directed by the parent body. Types include joint committees, standing committees and select or special committees. Conference committees have the duty of reconciling differences between House and Senate versions of bills. Most standing committees are divided into subcommittees appointed by their chairmen, which conduct hearings as directed and offer recommendations to their full committees. Only full committees, however, may report legislation to the floor. *See also Committee Membership; Committee Report; Conference Committee; Hearings; Standing Committees.*

committee membership Membership and rank on standing committees are largely determined by the seniority rule and the chairman, usually, is the majority member with the longest continuous service on the committee. The election of committee members takes place at the commencement of each two-year Congress. Formally, election is a function of the entire membership, but the actual choices tend to be made by each party's House or Senate caucus.

On each committee, majority and minority parties secure seats according to ratios agreed upon by the party leadership, roughly in proportion to their respective strengths in either house. The rule adopted by the 94th Congress, and continued by the 95th, gave the Democrats twice as many seats as the Republicans, plus one, on every House committee except Standards of Official Conduct and the Committee for the District of Columbia, which had two or three extra Democrats. The Senate has similar ratios, but a less rigid rule of proportion. In 1978, standing committees ranged in size from 12 to 55 members, the largest being the House Committee on Appropriations. *See also Conference Committee.*

committee of the whole To expedite the consideration of bills and resolutions, the House may resolve itself into the "Committee of the Whole House on the State of the Union." This parliamentary device allows it to act with a quorum of 100 members instead of the normally requisite 218. All measures on the Union Calendar (tax measures, appropriations and authorizations of payments) must have their first consideration in Committee of the Whole.

4

Measures debated in Committee of the Whole must have been reported by the appropriate committees and be on the Union Calendar. When the House sits as Committee of the Whole, a chairman takes the place of the Speaker and the measure is debated and amendments voted upon, to the extent permitted by the special ruling of the House Committee on Rules if as ordinarily the case, one has been granted. Upon completion of its deliberations, the Committee "rises," the Speaker resumes his place, and the full House hears and votes upon the Committee's recommendations. Prior to rules changes in 1971, voting positions taken in Committee of the Whole were never recorded.

committee report The findings and recommendations of a standing committee of either house after examining, amending and voting upon a referred measure; the act of bringing such a bill to the entire house for action on the floor. House and Senate committee reports are designated "H. Rept." or "S. Rept." respectively, and are numbered sequentially, with a prefix indicating the Congress. Some committee reports relate to special studies or investigations, rather than to specific legislation, although these may eventually give rise to legislation.

After examining a bill, the full committee may do one of several things. It may:

(1) Report the bill favorably, recommending ". . . that the bill do pass." After that, it may be the task of the chairperson to guide the bill through debate and passage.

(2) Refuse to report the bill; table it or let it die unreported. This happens to the majority of all bills, and many of them deserve their fate. If a committee pigeonholes a bill that a majority of the House wants to consider, it can be "blasted out" through the use of the discharge rule (*See Discharge a Committee*), but this isn't often successful.

(3) Report the bill with an unfavorable recommendation. This is rare, but it can happen when the committee senses a demand for the bill on the part of a number of members, and doesn't want to take responsibility for killing it.

(4) Report the bill in an amended form. Many bills are substantially altered in committee, and several bills on the same subject may be combined to produce one that can be reported with a recommendation.

(5) Report a "committee bill." In effect, this is an entirely new bill which the committee has created in place of the one or more submitted to it. The chairperson reports this new bill, and it goes on from there. House and Senate practices with respect to committee reports are generally similar.

Typically, a favorable committee report contains recommendations, an explanation of the committee's findings, the text of the bill with alterations indicated and a section-by-section analysis of its provisions. Space is allowed for additional, supplementary, and minority statements. Under recent legislation, cost estimates must be included. *See also Conference Committee; Intent of Congress.*

companion bills Bills in identical form introduced at approximately the same time in each house, in order to facilitate the legislative process. Because they must go through separate processes of mark-up and amendment, the companion bills may lose their identical character and acquire differences that must be resolved in conference.

concurrent resolution   Any matter affecting the operations or interests of both houses may become the subject of a concurrent resolution. While these must be passed by both houses, they do not become law. They are used to express the principles, opinions and purposes of the two houses, create joint committees, to establish budget ceilings under the recent Congressional Budget and Impoundment Control Act. If approved by both houses, they are published in the *United States Statutes at Large,* but are not submitted to the President. At times, concurrent resolutions are used to express the sense of Congress deploring some event or situation well outside the reach of the legislative power.

conference committee   A meeting of conferees or "managers" from each house, appointed to reconcile differences when a bill passed by one house is amended by the other, and the first does not concur in the amendments, or when versions of a bill passed by the respective houses differ in some substantial way. In a *simple conference* the conferees are bound by their instructions. In a *free conference* they may bargain, within limits. Since their deliberations are limited to areas of disagreement, they may not write and report new legislation.

A report is made if a majority from each house agree. Although the managers from each house meet as one committee, they are in effect two separate committees, each of which votes separately and acts by a majority vote. For this reason, the number of managers from each house is not particularly important. The report may recommend that either or both houses "recede" from their amendments, or "concur" in those of the other.

The house that agreed to the conference requested by the other is the first to act on the report. As the house voting first, it has three options: it may approve the report, reject it or send it back to conference. If it votes to approve, this action has the effect of discharging the conferees, with the result that the other house has only two options; to accept or reject the report. Conference report may not be amended on the floor.

Conferees, usually ranking members of the committees reporting the bills, are appointed by the presiding officers of their houses. Rules adopted at the beginning of the 94th Congress require conferences to be open, unless a majority of either chamber's conferees vote to close the session. A large part of all major legislation goes through conference and is revised, sometimes drastically. All appropriations bills go to conference, where the usual result is compromise between the higher and lower amounts proposed by the respective houses.

congress and session   A Congress extends over two calendar years, from January 3rd following the general elections ("unless Congress should by law appoint another date"), until final adjournment in September or October two years later, with breaks and recesses. Strictly speaking, Congress as such does not adjourn; the separate houses do so.

Each Congress is divided into two sessions, roughly corresponding to calendar years. Prior to the ratification of the Twentieth Amendment (1933), Congresses were divided into alternate "long" and "short" sessions. At present, they are of about the same duration, and being a congressman is a full-time job. Congresses have been numbered in sequence since the First Congress; sessions are designated as the first or second. Thus, Congressional documents are numbered by Congress and session, e.g., 94th Cong.,

2d Sess. might appear on a report. Public laws are numbered by the Congress in which they were enacted, plus a sequential number, e.g., P.L. 95–588, the last law of the 95th Congress. *See also Congress, Composition of House and Senate.*

congress, composition of house and senate

The House of Representatives comprises 435 members elected every two years from among the 50 states, their numbers being apportioned according to population, except that each state must have at least one representative. Beginning with 65 members in the First Congress (1789), the House reached 435 members in 1913. This number was made permanent by law in 1929, although it was increased temporarily in the 87th Congress to allow a member each from Alaska and Hawaii. The Senate is made up of 100 members, two from each state without regard for population. Presumably, this would be increased to 102 if the District of Columbia representation amendment, now pending, were to be ratified. Prior to the Seventeenth Amendment in 1913, senators were elected by their state legislatures, rather than by the voters directly.

A Resident Commissioner for Puerto Rico (elected for four years), and one delegate each from Guam, the Virgin Islands and the District of Columbia (elected for two years) are seated in the House of Representatives and complete the membership of Congress. They may introduce bills in the House and take part in debate, but not vote on the floor; however, they may vote in the House committees to which they are assigned.

Both senators and representatives must be residents of their states at the time of their election. In addition, a senator must be 30 years of age and must have been a United States citizen for at least nine years. Representatives must be 25 and have been citizens for seven years. *See also Congress, Terms of Office.*

congress, discipline and seating of members

Each house of Congress has authority to seat, refuse to seat, or discipline its members according to its own rules, within the general framework of the Constitution. While the two houses may censure or expel members for improper or disorderly conduct, they have done so rather infrequently. Between 1789 and 1975, seven senators and 18 representatives had been formally censured, and 15 senators and only three representatives expelled. Expulsion requires a two-thirds vote. Since censure may carry with it a loss of seniority, with a resultant loss of committee status and other attributes of power, it can have a serious effect on a member's subsequent political career.

With respect to seating, the Constitution states that each house "shall be the judge of the elections, returns, and qualifications of its own members." The power to exclude elected members was restricted by the Supreme Court in *Powell v. McCormack* (1969), and the rule today is that Congress must seat any member who is qualified and whose election was without irregularities. In a disputed election, either house may decide upon and seat a winner, declare the election void and require another, or leave the disputed seat vacant.

congress, terms of office

In accordance with the Twentieth Amendment (1933), which eliminated the alternate-year short session, members of both houses begin their terms on January 3rd of the year following the general election, regardless of whether Congress convenes on that date or somewhat later. Prior to 1933, terms began on March 3rd, which allowed the losers to hang on as lame ducks for two months—in a Congress to which they had not been elected.

Representatives are elected for two years, i.e., one Congress. Senators are elected for six years, their terms being staggered so that one-third of the Senate seats are contested in any general election. Senators are divided into classes in accordance with the closing dates of their terms, a practice that began with the First Congress (1789), when the newly-elected senators drew lots to determine whether their terms should end in two, four or six years. The terms of the senators from the same state do not end at the same time. Of the two senators from a state, the one elected first is referred to as the "senior" senator.

If a senator or representative dies, withdraws or is expelled, the governor of the state must call a special election, unless the state legislature has authorized him to appoint a successor, as most have. A member so elected or appointed serves for the balance of the term only.

congressional budget and impoundment control act of 1974

This measure (P.L. 93–344, which became fully effective in fiscal 1977, requires Congress to put a ceiling on spending and a floor under revenues in each fiscal year. It forces Congress to establish priorities and relate total spending to total revenue, instead of handling revenues and spending measures separately as in the past. The congressional budget process involves a series of deadlines, the most important of which are May 15, when Congress completes its first budget resolution with budget targets, and September 15, when the budget targets are replaced by budget ceilings in the second concurrent resolution. This series of actions, which does not require Presidential approval, establishes a congressional budget analogous to the Administration's budget. It should be noted that the congressional projections can be very different from those put forward by the Executive Branch.

For targeting purposes, the budget is divided into 16 functional categories, such as Income Security, Community Development, or General Government. Education is in the "500 series," or category, along with labor and welfare. A Joint Congressional Budget Office manages the technical complexities and serves as staff for the new House and Senate Budget Committees. The law also provides for congressional control over impoundments, *q.v. See also Full Funding.*

congressional districts

Political subdivisions of substantially equal population, each of which elects and is represented by one member of the House of Representatives, except in six smaller states, each of which has one representative at large (Alaska, Delaware, Nevada, North Dakota, Vermont and Wyoming). Districts are redrawn by the state legislatures, when necessary, to reflect internal shifts in population or changes in apportionment, *q.v.* District boundaries rarely coincide with those of any other political subdivision. A district may incorporate several communities, or a member may represent only part of a large city. Nationwide, the average district has a population of about 450,000 (on the basis of the 1970 census).

Efforts to improve the federal Apportionment Act of 1929 and 1941 have failed, with the result that redistricting has been governed, to a great extent, by decisions of the Supreme Court. While the Court has demanded high standards of numerical equality, it has neglected other criteria such as compactness, contiguity and homogeneity in drawing district lines. Typically, the absolute deviation in population between the largest and smallest districts in any state is less than one percent.

congressional oversight

The Legislative Reorganization Act of 1946 provides that each standing committee of either house "shall exercise continuous watchfulness of the execution by the administrative agencies concerned of any laws, the subject matter of which is within the jurisdiction of such committee . . ." Each committee reports on its oversight activities at the end of each Congress. This provision has expanded the investigative function of Congress and strengthened and legitimized its "watchdog" role. Congress is assisted in its oversight function by the General Accounting Office.

Congressional Record

Proceedings of both houses have been reported since 1873 in the *Congressional Record*, issued daily by the Government Printing Office while Congress is in session. Between 1830 and 1873, Congress was covered by the privately-owned *Congressional Globe*. The *Record* reports debate in full, together with speeches, motions, all recorded votes and the major steps in parliamentary procedure.

Members are allowed to edit their statements and make substantial additions, with the result that remarks reported by the press may not show up in the *Record*, and some things may appear in the *Record* that didn't really get said on the floor. Since March 1, 1978, these unspoken speeches and interpolations have been marked off between "bullet" symbols. A "Daily Digest" section summarizes proceedings in each house and outlines the legislative program for the next day. An "Extension of Remarks" section allows members to develop their thoughts on issues and include extraneous matter from many sources. The Constitution requires each house to maintain a journal containing its minutes. These documents, less well known than the *Record*, have been maintained since the First Congress.

congressional veto

Something of a misnomer, since regulations, rather than bills, are subject to nullification under Congressional veto provisions. The so-called "veto" clauses, estimated to appear in at least a hundred recent enactments, range from a simple requirement that an agency's proposed regulations be sent to Congress for review, to a requirement for congressional approval before a regulation can go into effect.

Congressional interest in veto provisions appears to reflect public displeasure with the "fourth branch of government," the federal bureaucracy. So far, no general veto law has been enacted, although several measures that would give Congress authority to disapprove almost any agency regulation have been proposed in recent years. Opposition by the leadership and important committee chairmen has been sufficient to defeat them.

consent calendar

One of the five legislative calendars, or agendas, of the House. Bills may be shifted to this calendar from the House or Union calendars if they are considered to be noncontroversial. Bills on the Consent Calendar are called on the first and third Mondays of each month. On the first call, consideration may be blocked by one member and the bill carried over. On the second call, the bill is stricken and reverts to the House or Union Calendars if two or more members object. If no objection is made, the bill is passed by unanimous consent without debate. To be certain that bills on the Consent Calendar are actually minor and noncontroversial, they are examined by six "official objectors," three each from the majority and minority parties.

continuing resolution　It sometimes happens that a fiscal year comes to an end before Congress has completed all of the appropriations bills awaiting passage. To keep the government in business, Congress then passes a joint resolution "continuing appropriations" for the affected agencies, usually at the existing level of funding. *Compare Supplemental Appropriation.*

co-sponsor　Members of either house who join in the sponsorship of a bill, thus signifying their support, at least at the moment. Originally, the House did not permit co-sponsorship. In 1967, the House voted to allow co-sponsors to the limit of 25, a rule often circumvented by introducing the same bill more than once. Also, members may submit identical bills when they wish to support a measure, but do not want to become identified with other members whose party or political philosophy may be different.

deferral　An Executive Branch action, or inaction, which temporarily withholds or delays the obligation or expenditure of budget authority. In effect, a deferral puts off the spending of appropriated money until later in the fiscal year. Under the Congressional Budget and Impoundment Control Act of 1974, the President must explain any proposed deferral in a special message to Congress. A deferral takes effect automatically unless either house objects to it within 45 days. A deferral may not continue past the end of a fiscal year.

deficit　The amount by which a government's budget outlays exceed its budget receipts for a given period. Deficits are financed primarily by borrowing from the public. The opposite situation creates a surplus.

discharge a committee　"Blasting" a bill out of committee. The release of a committee from further jurisdiction over a legislative proposal, with the effect of bringing the matter to the floor. This procedure, designed to prevent a committee from "smothering' a bill that the members in general wish to take action on, may be initiated by any member of the House if a committee does not report a bill within 30 days, but it isn't easy.

In the House, a discharge petition requires the signatures of a majority of members (218). Then, after a seven-day waiting period, any member who signed may move to discharge. If the motion is carried, the bill comes to the floor. Being privileged, it receives immediate consideration. If a request for a special ruling on a bill by the House Rules Committee has been held up for seven days, any member may move to discharge that committee. At times, a committee may be discharged by unanimous consent of the House, usually to bring some noncontroversial matter to the floor. In the Senate, a motion to discharge a committee may be offered by any member. It is carried by a majority vote.

due process　Originally, a principle derived from the common law, restraining the executive branch from depriving persons of life, liberty or property by arbitrary means outside the normal course of the law. In the United States, the principle is embodied in many provisions of the Bill of Rights. Due process appears in the Fifth Amendment as a restraint on the federal government; in the Fourteenth Amendment as a restraint on the states.

Procedural due process governs administrative and judicial actions, which must be predictable, even-handed and available to all. No action in the nature of punishment or correction may be taken until an appropriate finding of guilt or noncompliance has been made in the normally prescribed manner. *Substantive due process* means that the courts will not enforce arbitrary or unjust provisions of any law under which a person has been tried. The Supreme Court has used the concept of due process to strengthen other guarantees under the Constitution, and has assimilated most of the provisions of the first eight Amendments into the Fourteenth Amendment, so as to bar their infringement by the states.

election days
By law, national general elections are held on the Tuesday after the first Monday in November, in even-numbered years. Although most state elections take place on the same day, a few states hold elections in November in the odd-numbered years.

engrossed bill
The final, correct copy of a bill as passed by one house, together with amendments, attested by the signature of the Secretary of the Senate or the Clerk of the House, and ready to be messaged to the other for its action.

enrolled bill
A bill ready for submission to the President, having been passed in an identical form by both houses, and signed first by the Speaker of the House and then by the President of the Senate. An enrolled bill is printed on parchment paper and examined for accuracy by the Committee on House Administration. Subsequently, the text of the bill serves as photoelectric offset copy for the printing of an accurate slip law. After signing, or passage without signature, the document is sent to the General Services Administration for numbering and is deposited in the National Archives.

executive calendar
The Senate, which has but one calendar or agenda for all legislative proposals, uses the non-legislative Executive Calendar for Presidential matters such as nominations and treaties. The Senate's legislative calendar is known as the Calendar of Bills and Resolutions.

executive session
A meeting of a House or Senate committee (rarely, the whole chamber), from which the press and public are excluded, but in which the testimony of witnesses may be received. Recently adopted "open meeting" policies in both houses have tended to diminish the use of executive sessions.

expenditure
The spending of funds, as distinguished from their appropriation. Expenditures are made by federal departments and agencies, i.e., the Executive Branch, while appropriations are the work of Congress. Expenditures and appropriations are not identical in any given year, since appropriating action may have taken place one, two or more years earlier.

extension of remarks
Both houses rather freely grant their members "leave to publish" undelivered speeches, communications, reprinted matter and other extraneous materials in the *Congressional Record's* "Extension of Remarks" section. The resulting anthology of Americana reveals much about the tastes, interests and problems of congressmen and their constituents.

Federal Register
This periodical, now a daily, began publication in May, 1936, as the official notice board for agencies in the Executive Branch. Its importance was increased by the Administrative Procedures Act of 1946, which required all proposed and final regulations, notices of intended rulemaking, executive orders, reorganization plans, program deadlines and other material of importance to persons who deal with the federal government. Regulations gain the force of law upon publication in the *Federal Register*, which is keyed to the permanent *Code of Federal Regulations*. The *Register* also includes Presidential papers, the titles and numbers of newly-enacted public

laws, and various notices and findings by regulatory and other federal agencies.

filibuster Delaying tactics employed on the floor by a minority seeking to block a vote or compel a majority to modify its legislative program, usually by prolonged speech-making and dilatory motions. Until recently, Senate rules permitting unlimited debate favored the filibuster and made its termination by cloture almost impossible. Between 1917 and 1975, the Senate required the votes of two-thirds of the senators present and voting to cut off debate. In 1975, this rule was changed to provide that debate could be cut off by the vote of 60 senators, rather than 67 as under the prior rule, if all 100 were present and voting. The filibuster has been defended as a vital protection for minority rights, and as a defense for the small states against the larger ones, heavily represented in the other chamber. In the House of Representatives, unlike the Senate, the rules make real filibuster hard to sustain, although a "minifilibuster" can be staged by offering amendments, insisting on points of order and demanding roll call votes; all dilatory tactics that the Speaker usually quells.

fiscal year For planning and budgetary purposes, the financial year of the federal government does not coincide with the calendar year. Between 1921 and 1976, the fiscal year ran from July 1 to June 30. To meet the additional procedural demands of the new budget cycle under the Congressional Budget and Impoundment Control Act the beginning of the fiscal year was advanced three months, with the result that the 1977 fiscal year began October 1, 1976 and ended September 30, 1977. The three-month hiatus between the end of the old 1976 fiscal year and the beginning of fiscal 1977 constituted the "transition quarter." A fiscal year carries the date of the calendar year in which it ends.

floor action Action taken by a quorum of the full membership of either house on a bill or other measure as reported by a committee. Also, action by the Committee of the Whole in the House. Subject to the rules, members may introduce amendments, enter into debate, seek in various ways to prevent or promote the passage of a measure, and vote on its passage. In the House, floor action may be circumscribed by special rulings of the Committee on Rules.

A "floor fight" is said to take place when partisans and opponents of a controversial measure make use of carefully-concerted political and parliamentary tactics to gain their ends in a close contest. The custom of bringing bowie knives and loaded canes to the chambers was abandoned some years ago, but of procedural ingenuity there is no end.

floor leader A member designated by his party's caucus to take charge of party interests during legislative sessions. He may plan the course of debate, direct the submission of amendments, determine the order in which members of his party shall speak, and, through the whips, strive to maintain party solidarity. In the Senate, the floor leaders from the two parties largely decide when debate shall be closed and a vote taken. The Majority and Minority Leaders are recognized officers of the two houses, with special staff assistance and higher salaries than the members at large.

franking privilege The right of members of Congress to send official mail free of charge within covers bearing their signatures in facsimile in place of stamps. Members receive up to 40,000 public document envelopes per month for franked mail. In addition, each member has substantial allowances for telephone calls and special delivery mail, and $5,000 annually for the publication of newsletters and the like. House and Senate have somewhat different rules on franked mail. Changes instituted in the 95th Congress might save some money by increasing the use of third class for some franked matter, but will be likely to increase the actual volume, particularly on the Senate side.

full funding Funding of federal programs through the appropriation of amounts substantially equal to the ceilings specified in the authorizing legislation, unless urgent considerations make such funding levels inadvisable. The adoption of the principle of full funding would put an end to the irresponsible practice of authorizing sums not seriously expected to be made available, and shift the burden of proof to any legislator who might propose appropriations significantly below authorized levels.

germaneness House rules require that amendments must be relevant to the subject matter of the bill involved. Both houses object to the attachment of substantive or authorizing amendments to an appropriations bill, or "legislating in a money bill."

The Senate's germaneness rule is limited to general appropriations bills, bills considered under cloture and proceedings under agreement to limit debate. Otherwise, senators are free to attach all manner of non-germane "riders." Prior to the Legislative Reorganization Act of 1970, the House was forced to accept such amendments or reject the bill. Today, the House may take a separate vote on any Senate amendment that would be non-germane under House rules.

hearings If a bill is of sufficient importance, or is controversial or complex, the committee to which it was referred may hold public hearings at which it will receive oral and written testimony from specialists, government officials, members of Congress or the public. Witnesses may volunteer their testimony, appear by request or be subpoenaed. Hearings may range from perfunctory, with a few witnesses appearing briefly before two or three committee members, to full-scale performances with heavy press coverage, lasting days or weeks.

Ordinarily, witnesses are expected to file their written statements prior to the hearing, and to limit their oral presentations to five minutes. In the House, each committee member is limited to five minutes in which to interrogate witnesses, until each member has been able to ask questions. A committee may hear testimony, but not vote, in the absence of a quorum. Transcripts must be made available for public inspection at the committee's office. Whether the proceedings will be printed in full is at the discretion of the committee.

hold harmless A regulation or statutory provision, usually financial in nature, providing that current beneficiaries under a specified grant-in-aid program will not suffer as a result of changes in law, regulations, formulas or funding levels. Payments under a hold harmless provision may receive a high priority. A form of "grandfather clause," also called a "save harmless" provision.

House The House of Representatives or, in lower case usage, either body or "house" of a bicameral legislature. "Chamber" may be a synonym, or it may refer to the actual meeting room of either house.

House calendar One of the five calendars or agendas of the House, listing bills that do not raise revenue or directly or indirectly appropriate money or property.

impoundment A general term referring to the withholding of budget authority from obligation, through deferral or rescission. On the federal level, impoundment amounts to a refusal on the part of the Executive to make use of money appropriated by the legislature, thus appearing to thwart the intent of Congress. This, incidentally, is one of the few situations not anticipated by the authors of the Constitution. In their experience, the executive—the Crown—had never been known to refuse appropriated funds. President Nixon's use of impoundment to achieve supposed economies led to the passage of the Congressional Budget and Impoundment Control Act of 1974, which gives Congress the final word on this practice.

Intent of Congress What they actually meant when they passed the law. The interpretation of a statute is faciliated by reference to the text of debate on the floor, committee reports, conference reports and other congressional documents serving to enlarge upon the statutory language and provide background information. Such materials lack the direct force of law, but are persuasive in the courts. Evidence of the intent of Congress can be decisive in the development of regulations, as well. In recent years, slip laws have included a "legislative history" note that provides reference to House, Senate and conference reports, and to debate in the *Congressional Record*.

item veto In some states, the governor may veto portions of an appropriation bill, and, in a few instances, other bills, without invalidating the remainder of the legislation. The President, who lacks this power, must accept or veto a bill in its entirety. This makes it possible to "veto proof" a bit of legislation by sending it up as a rider on some other bill that the President will be reluctant to veto, for political or practical reasons.

joint committee A committee made up of member of both houses, usually with investigative functions or operational responsibilities affecting both. Standing joint committees include the Joint Committee on Economics, the Joint Committee on Internal Revenue Taxation, and committees on printing and the Library of Congress, fewer than in the past. The Joint Committee on Defense Production and the once-powerful Joint Committee on Atomic Energy were not funded after fiscal 1977. The Joint Committee on Congressional Operations has become a House select committee with similar functions. None of the joint committees has authority to report legislation.

joint resolution Joint resolutions originate in either house and not, as the name suggests, jointly in both houses. In modern times, there is little distinction between a bill and a joint resolution, although the latter tend to be used for unusual or temporary matters, such as appropriating funds for the Presidential inauguration or to correct errors in previously passed statutes.

Bills and joint resolutions, with one exception, pass through the same procedural steps and create public law. A joint resolution, *not* signed by the President, is used when an amendment to the Constitution is proposed. A Joint resolution originating in the House is designated "H.J. Res.," plus a sequential number. A Senate joint resolution is designated "S.J. Res.," and numbered.

law (1) A bill or joint resolution that has been passed by both houses, signed by the President, passed over his veto or allowed to become effective without his signature. "Act" and "statute" are approximate synonyms. (2)

An order, ruling or regulation issued by a duly empowered agency pursuant to a legislative enactment. Hence the expression, "having the force of law." (3) The entire body of authoritative rules governing a political community, whether legislative, judicial, administrative or customary in origin, together with the principles of justice and propriety applied to their development and enforcement.

legislative day The official, rather than the calendar day, extending from the time either house meets until its next adjournment. In the House, where each day's work usually ends with an adjournment, legislative days and calendar days tend to coincide. In the Senate, a legislative day may extend over several calendar days.

lobbyist A person who seeks, either as an individual or an agent, to make members of Congress aware of the needs and interests of various elements in American society, and of the probable consequences of policy alternatives, so as to influence the development of legislation. A lobbyist or his organization may provide useful expertise in the drafting of bills and amendments, the conduct of investigations or the management of campaigns. The development of testimony and the recruitment of witnesses for committee hearings are important functions of the lobbyist. "Agency lobbying" directed to the Executive Branch is similar, except that it has to do with the development of regulations and program priorities, rather than legislation, and is of equal importance. The other important function of the lobbyist is the political education and coordination of his constituency group, so that its members can take a more effective and responsible part in the development of legislation and policy.

Legitimate lobbying, which provides congressmen with vital information and links them with the persons they serve, falls within the constitutional right of citizens to "petition for the redress of grievances." Although current laws designed to curb abuses in lobbying are widely understood to be inadequate, Congress has found it difficult to enact suitable controls over this basically necessary activity.

local entitlement A system of allocation under which federal funds are distributed to local units of government, such as school districts, according to local criteria and without the intervention of other levels of government. Under local entitlement, a school district can be relatively certain of its share of a given appropriation, and the state level is eliminated or reduced to a ministerial role.

maintenance of effort Federal grant-in-aid programs ordinarily require the recipient of funds to use the money to supplement rather than to supplant the financial contributions they would otherwise be making on behalf of the activity supported, and to maintain the level of support that existed prior to the federal grant. Particular years, populations or other criteria may be specified for purposes of comparison.

majority A *simple majority* is made up of more than half of those present and voting. In this glossary, "majority" usually refers to a simple majority. An *absolute majority* comprises more than half of those entitled to vote on a question, whether present or not. In the Senate, an absolute majority would be 51; in the House, 218. *See also Plurality; Quorum.*

majority leader A senior member elected by the caucus of the party in nominal control of either house to take charge of party strategy on the floor and otherwise

15

coordinate its efforts. The Senate majority leader controls the allocation of time for debate and holds a position of power. In the House, the majority leader tends to become the principal assistant to the Speaker, who is the party's effective leader on that side of Congress. The majority and minority leaders may also be called "floor leaders."

mark-up of a bill   In either house, a committee or subcommittee session in which a bill is reviewed in detail, with language being added or deleted by amendment to meet the needs and objections of the committee members, usually after testimony has been taken in hearings. At this stage, the bill may be printed in expanded format with numbered lines to facilitate discussion and revision. If the bill is extensively revised or completely rewritten, the committee or subcommittee may order a "clean bill" printed, which will be reported under a new number.

Until recently, many mark-ups were held behind closed doors, with the press and public excluded. After the adoption of open meeting rules (House, 1973; Senate, 1975), open mark-ups became usual. There is reason to think that much of the close bargaining that characterized closed mark-ups is being done through telephone calls and informal caucuses, and that a large part of the traditional secrecy has been preserved.

matching grants   Many categorical grant-in-aid programs require that every federal dollar be matched with one or more dollars from some non-federal source, and prospective grantees may be required to show that such funds are available.

A variation on the matching principle is *cost sharing*, wherein the grantee is expected to make some contribution to the total expense of a project. This may be nominal, or it may be a significant percentage of project cost. In other instances, the cost sharing requirement may be met by a contribution in kind, such as the provision of space, staff or materials.

member of Congress   Both senators and representatives are properly termed members of Congress, since the Congress comprises both bodies, but the term most frequently refers to representatives. The related term "congressman" almost always means a member of the House.

minority leader   In either house, performs duties of floor leader for the minority party.

motion   Parliamentary request by a member for a substantive or procedural action, usually becoming effective upon minority vote, or with the approval of the presiding officer.

obligation   A commitment made by a federal agency to pay out money for products, services, grants or other purposes, as distinct from actual payments. Obligations incurred by an agency may not be larger than its budget authority.

original bill   Bills to carry out the recommendations of the President are introduced, as a rule, by the chairmen of the committees, that have jurisdiction over their subject matter. At times, the committees themselves may introduce and report "original bills" to carry out the Administration's program of legislation.

party caucus   A closed meeting of the members of each party in each house. Caucuses meet in January just before each Congress and session to make organizational decisions, and occasionally during a session. In recent years, the Republicans have referred to their caucuses as *party conferences*. Many decisions formally attributed to the full membership of the respective houses, such as committee membership and the election of the Speaker of the House and other leadership, are largely determined by committees in the party caucuses.

Each party organization has permanent steering committees, policy committees and campaign committees with professional staffs and regular publications. In addition, each party maintains a research staff (Democratic Study Group; Republican Study Committee) in both houses, to supply members with legislative information and policy materials. Although the party caucus cannot, ultimately, compel member acceptance of its decision, it continues to be a powerful instrument of party discipline and coordination.

plurality The margin by which the vote received by the leading candidate exceeds the vote for the next highest candidate, in a field of three or more candidates. While a plurality may be sufficient to carry an election, it may be substantially less than a majority.

pocket veto If Congress should adjourn during the ten-day period given the President for the consideration of an enrolled bill, he may withhold his signature and allow the bill to die, without explanation. If Congress remains in session, or should reconvene before the end of the ten-day period, the bill becomes law if the President does not sign. Federal courts have held that the pocket veto does not operate during short recesses.

point of order A question or objection raised by a member in either chamber as to the propriety of a motion or proceeding under the rules. The presiding officer must rule immediately, subject to an appeal to the members on the floor. Order is restored by suspending proceedings until the house conforms its conduct to the rules. At times, "point of order" has been used to delay or confuse the business of the house. Points of order may also be raised in committee. In the House, a special ruling of the House Committee on Rules may limit the number of points of order that may be raised in debate on a particular bill. When a chamber is in an uproar, which can happen, a member may raise a "point of no order."

powers of Congress The Constitution defines the powers of Congress in Article I, Section 8. Included are the power to assess and collect taxes, often called the chief power; to regulate commerce, both interstate and foreign; to coin money; to establish post offices and post roads; to establish courts inferior to the Supreme Court; to declare war; to raise and maintain an army and navy. Congress is further empowered "To provide for calling forth the Militia to execute the laws of the Union, suppress Insurrections and repel Invasions;" and "To make all laws which shall be necessary and proper for carrying into execution the foregoing Powers, and all other Powers vested by this Constitution in the Government of the United States, or in any Department or Officer thereof."

In most respects coequal, the Senate and House have certain special powers reserved to each of them under the Constitution. A large number of Presidential nominations to appointive office require the consent of a majority of the Senate, and all treaties must be approved by two-thirds of the Senate. All revenue bills must originate in the House. In practice, the House also originates appropriation bills, although this is not specified by the Constitution. Both houses act in impeachment proceedings, the House having the power of impeachment (analogous to indictment), while the Senate sits as a court to try impeachments. Finally, if no person receives a majority of votes for President in the electoral college, the final election is decided by the House, with each state having one vote. This situation, which the framers of the Constitution thought would be frequent, has actually occurred only twice: in 1801, when the House chose Jefferson over Burr; and in 1825, when John Quincy Adams was selected rather than Andrew Jackson.

President of the Senate

The Vice President serves as presiding officer of the Senate. Not a member, he votes only in the event of a tie.

President *pro tempore*

The presiding officer of the Senate in the absence of the Vice President. The practice, for some time, has been to elect to this post the majority party senator with the longest continuous service. In the event of his own absence, the President *pro tempore* will appoint an acting *pro tem*. In the early days, the President *pro tempore* was held to act for the occasion only. Since 1976, they have served "until the Senate otherwise ordered." One senator often holds the position through several sessions.

Presidential documents

Presidential speeches, news conferences, messages and other items made public by the White House are published in the *Weekly Compilation of Presidential Documents* and cumulated annually in the *Public Papers of the Presidents*. Presidential proclamations and Executive Orders having the force of law also appear in the daily *Federal Register*.

public laws, names and numbering

Most recent statutes include an official "short title" by which they may be cited. In addition, many laws have acquired unofficial or popular names such as the Taft-Hartley Act or the Homestead Laws. There is no requirement that a law have an official title. Many of our early statutes did not, and the practice has been neglected from time to time, even recently. The two enactments creating the Impact Aid program (which itself has had several names) were untitled, and are cited as P.L. 81–815 and P.L. 81–874. Well-known bills are likely to be named after their sponsors, even before they are enacted. The official title of a *bill*, however, is a brief descriptive phrase reading "An Act to establish (authorize, provide) . . ., and other purposes." Printing this title in the *Congressional Record* carries out the first of the three parliamentary "readings" needed before a bill can pass.

Where substantial new authorizing language is added to an existing law by amendment, the new section may contain an official title for citation as an act in its own right. For example, Title V of the Higher Education Act of 1963 (added by amendment in 1967) may be cited as the Education Professions Development Act. Public laws are designated by the Congress in which they are passed, plus a sequential number indicating the order of enactment, e.g., P.L. 94–588, the last public law of the 94th Congress. Enactment refers to a point at which a law is signed by the President, passed by veto override, or allowed to take effect without signature.

quorum

The minimum number of members required to be present for action to be taken in a legislative body. In both House and Senate, a simple majority of members constitutes a quorum (51 in the Senate; 218 in the House, if there are no vacancies). A quorum is 100 when the House sits as Committee of the Whole, *q.v.* If a quorum is not present, a house may adjourn, refrain from taking action or direct its Sergeant-at-Arms to round up some of the absentees. The presence of a quorum may be ascertained by a roll call. In 1890, Speaker of the House Reed instituted the practice of directing the Clerk to add to the role the names of those present in the chamber but refusing to answer ("disappearing quorum"). In committee, where a majority also constitutes a quorum, less than a quorum may meet and hear testimony, but not vote.

quorum call   When a vote is to be taken, members are summoned by a system of lights and bells in their respective office buildings.

readings of a bill   English parliamentary practice, copied by our Congress, required that a bill should be read three times in the chamber before it could be passed. The printing and distribution of bills, and the press of business, has made this practice obsolete. Today, a bill has its first reading when it is introduced and printed by title in the *Congressional Record*. The second reading comes on the floor after general debate. The bill may be read section-by-section, and amendments may be offered to a section when it is read, to the extent permitted by the rule granted by the Rules Committee, if in the House. The third reading, usually by title, follows floor action on amendments, after which the "question is taken" on its passage.

recess   In contrast with adjournment, a recess does not end the legislative day and does not interfere with the continuation of business. The Senate makes frequent use of the recess, thus extending its legislative day over several calendar days. The House originally adjourns from day to day.

recommit a bill   A motion made on the floor to send a bill back to the committee reporting it, usually with the effect of killing the bill. In the House, this motion must be made by a member opposed to the bill. The motion may direct the committee to report the bill with certain specified amendments by a stated date, or it may call for further study. After the previous question has been ordered on the passage of a bill or joint resolution, it is in order to make one motion to recommit; a last chance for the opposition to prevail before the final vote.

regions and regionalization   Many federal agencies have found it appropriate to conduct a part of their business through regional offices, dividing the country into from five to a dozen geographical areas in accordance with their missions. Under President Nixon, a partially successful effort was made to conform agency regions to nine (later ten) standard areas. Properly implemented, the policy can improve agency accessibility and responsiveness.

Regionalization refers to the policy of transferring much program responsibility from the national to the regional level. Instead of serving as "field offices," the regions now take on much of the decision-making that was done in Washington. Because Washington is not really able to let go of its responsibilities under law, this policy may increase bureaucracy by interposing another level between programs and their clients. This trend has been reversed in recent years, and normal patterns of communication and authority are being reestablished.

regulation   A rule made by an executive officer charged with the administration of a law, for the guidance of his agency and the persons and organizations affected. An official interpretation of a statute, detailing the steps to be taken in its administration and enforcement. Authorizing acts usually direct the agency head to develop implementing regulations.

Under the Administrative Procedures Act and Section 431 of the General Education Provisions Act, new or changed regulations must be published in the *Federal Register* and the public given time and opportunity to comment. The stages in the promulgation of a regulation are: (1) notice of intent to publish new or changed regulations, (2) proposed regulations, (3) revision following comment, and (4) final regulations. Only the latter have legal force.

rescission Legislation enacted by Congress at the request of the President to cancel some previously-granted budget authority. Rescission amounts to taking back part of an appropriation and, possibly, terminating some authorized activity. Under the 1974 Congressional Budget and Impoundment Control Act, the President must submit a message explaining his reasons for the proposed rescission.

If Congress does not approve the action within 45 days, the money may be expended. Small rescissions brought about by changed conditions are rather common. This may be contrasted with deferral, *q.v.*, which takes effect immediately and remains in effect unless Congress objects. Deferral postpones spending; rescission cancels part of an appropriation.

revenue sharing The practice of redistributing or returning a part of the tax income of the federal government to the states and localities, in such a way as to offset fiscal inequities and compensate for relative declines in tax resources at the lower levels of government.

The rationale for revenue sharing is three-fold: (1) Federal tax receipts, based on the income tax, are believed to grow more rapidly than the economy as a whole, whereas state and local receipts, dependent on sales and property taxes, tend to lag behind the general economy and behind the cost of providing governmental services. (2) For various reasons, many areas do not have the tax resources to support services such as education at acceptable levels. (3) It is believed that fiscal assistance through revenue sharing serves to return decision-making responsibility to the state and local levels, since the uses of the money are not mandated.

rider An amendment, usually irrelevant, added to a bill so that opponents will have to accept the additional language or forego the bill; a device to embarrass the Administration or secure the passage of a measure that could not pass by itself. At times, a provision that the President would prefer to reject can be "veto-proofed" by attaching it to an important bill that he cannot afford to veto. Riders are sometimes added to appropriations bills, in disregard of House and Senate rules against "legislating in a money bill." Since 1970, the House has been able to take a separate vote on Senate riders that would be non-germane under the rules of the House.

roll call Calling the names of members on the floor or in committees for a recorded vote or to ascertain the existence of a quorum.

rule (1) A decision of the House Committee on Rules which, if adopted by a majority vote of the House membership, governs the manner in which a reported bill is to be debated and amended on the floor. (2) A standing regulation governing proceedings in either house, published in its compilation of rules and precedents. Rules in this sense may be created or modified by resolutions in either house, and reflect years of parliamentary experience.

Within the general framework of the Constitution, which offers little guidance for the internal operations of Congress, each house is free to adopt its own rules, elect its own officers, and seat and discipline its members.

The House of Representatives adopts its rules anew when it reorganizes at the beginning of a new Congress. Since the Senate is organized as a continuing body, its rules are regarded as permanent.

select or special committee

A committee created by a simple resolution in either house, the jurisdiction of which is limited to investigating and reporting on a specific subject, and which expires when that service is completed. This impermanence is relative, however. Some select committees have been in existence for at least a decade. In the House, a select or special committee must be reestablished each Congress. Some authorities find special committees to be the more mission-oriented, while others see no distinction.

seniority rule

With respect to committee assignments, the custom in both houses is that a member who has served on a committee in previous Congresses is entitled to reappointment, and to enjoy rank in accordance with his years of continuous service. The majority member with the longest service is likely to be named chairman, although the party caucus doesn't always follow this rule. Subcommittee assignments and chairmanships, usually governed by committee chairmen, are normally based on seniority together with the preferences of the members. Among members who entered Congress at the same time, weight is given to previous service in elective office (as governor, state legislator, or member of the opposite house; now lower).

simple resolution

Either house may initiate and adopt a simple resolution concerning its own internal operations without the action of the other and, of course, without Presidential approval. Simple resolutions are designated "H. Res." or "S. Res.," with sequential numbers. If adopted, they are published in the *Congressional Record* and entered in the *Journal*.

Speaker of the House

Presiding officer of the House of Representatives. The Speaker rules on questions of order; appoints chairmen of the Committee of the Whole; signs acts, warrants, subpoenas and orders of the House; appoints conference and special committees; and appoints the parlimentarian and other officials. Prior to the "congressional revolution" of 1910–11, the Speaker appointed all standing committees and was chairman of the Committee on Rules, a combination that went far to justify Speaker Reed's observation that his position was the "highest in the gift of the republic."

Unlike the presiding officer of the Senate, the Speaker is an elected member and is leader of his party on his side of Congress. He may vote, but by custom rarely does so except to break or create a tie. The Speaker is elected by the House (in actuality, by the caucus or the majority party) at the opening of each Congress. He may designate any member to preside in his absence.

standing committees

Permanent committees provided by House and Senate rules, and having among them explicit jurisdiction over nearly the whole possible subject matter of legislation. The Legislative Reorganization Acts of 1946 and 1970 reduced the number of House and Senate standing committees from 48 and 33 to 21 and 17 respectively.

sunset law

A law requiring specified agencies, or groups of agencies with related functions, to terminate their existence at the end of a stated period and then justify their continuation before Congress. Closely related to zero-base budgeting.

sunshine law

A law or regulation requiring the deliberations of a legislative or admin-

21

istrative body to be open to the press and public, unless considerations of privacy or security dictate otherwise. Committee meetings in the House and Senate have been open since 1973 and 1975, respectively. A "government in the sunshine" law signed in 1976, P.L. 94-409, applies to agencies headed by commissioners appointed by the President, thus including most of the powerful regulatory agencies. "Open record" laws require the transcripts, but not the meetings themselves, to be open to the public. At present, every state has an open meeting or an open record law.

supplemental appropriation An appropriation passed out of the normal order (1) to defray unanticipated or extraordinary expenditures, or (2) to fund activities authorized too late for the normal budgetary deadlines. Unlike continuing resolutions, supplementals are public laws and require the signature of the President—who may have requested the money.

table a measure A majority can suspend consideration of any pending measure by a motion to table. Tabling usually amounts to a final and adverse disposition of a bill. When a measure is tabled, a vote of two-thirds is required to return it to the floor. An amendment may be tabled without prejudice to the bill itself. Tabling may also take place in committee, with the same fatal effect. The Senate allows a motion to "lay on the table," a less drastic action which has the effect of preserving the bill for later consideration.

unanimous consent In either house, noncontroversial motions, amendments or bills may be passed without a vote if no member raises an objection from the floor. "Without objection" is a synonym for unanimous consent. The same practice exists in committee deliberations.

United States Code An official compilation of the permanent and general laws of the United States, codified under 50 titles. The first six deal with general and political matters. The remaining 44 are alphabetized from Agriculture to War. The *Code* is supplemented after each session of Congress and revised every six years. The privately-distributed *United States Code Annotated* combines the same statutory materials with historical notes, court decisions and rulings of the Attorney General.

upper and lower houses The Senate and the House of Representatives, respectively. Inasmuch as the houses of Congress are equal in dignity and in their ability to initiate, debate and act upon legislation, many authorities consider it improper to refer to them as "upper" and "lower" houses, particularly since their members are now elected by the same body of voters, without regard to social or other distinctions. The authors of the Constitution apparently relied on the Senate, stable and propertied, to curb the democratic ebullience of the House—but that was then.

veto The right of the President to return a bill or joint resolution unsigned to the house of origin, with a written statement of his objections to it, within ten days of its delivery to him after passage by Congress, thereby preventing it from becoming law unless it can be re-passed over his veto. The ten-day period excludes Sundays and national holidays, but not Saturdays.

veto override If the President returns a bill unsigned and with objections stated in writing within ten days of its delivery to him, it does not become law unless Congress can re-pass it with a recorded vote of two-thirds (of a quorum) in both houses. The bill is sent by the President to the house in which it originated. Privileged, it is voted upon immediately and, if the requisite vote is obtained, is referred to the other house for its action. If not successful in both houses, the bill is dead.

voting procedures The House now uses three methods for taking votes on the floor. In committee, voting practices are limited, usually, to voice votes and roll calls. According to most committee rules, roll call or recorded votes may be demanded by any member. The voting procedures used by the House are as follows:

(1) *Voice votes* are the most frequent. All those in favor answer "aye," in chorus, followed by the "no" votes, also in unison. The presiding officer decides "by ear."

(2) If any member thinks the Speaker has erred in judging a voice vote, he may demand a *standing vote*, technically known as a "division of the House." All in favor, and then all opposed, stand and are counted by the Clerk.

(3) A *roll call vote*, also known as a *recorded vote*, may be demanded by one-fifth of the members present (at least 44).

whip The whips serve as first assistants to the majority and minority leaders in both houses. Along with other duties, they remind members to be present for votes, arrange pairs, conciliate disaffected members and keep the leadership informed about the attitudes of the rank and file. In today's House and Senate, the whips offices have important information functions, issuing notices, schedules and policy materials to the members of their parties. In the House, the Majority Whip has the assistance of three deputy whips.

zero-base budgeting Experience shows that the natural tendency of bureaucracies is to persist, and that change in bureaucratic structures, to the extent that it happens at all, takes the form of growth and expansion, with each year's budget request adding something to the past year's expenditure level. Very often, this takes place without any real changes in an agency's services, either in kind or quality.

Zero-base budgeting proposes to attack the problem of bureaucratic expansion by forcing each agency of government to come before the appropriate legislative body and justify its entire existence, not merely its proposed increase for the coming year. At this point, each agency would start over at the beginning, or "zero base," with no certainty of continuation on any level.

Most federal zero-base proposals call for program review by functional areas, such as education, welfare or law enforcement, so that Congress will be able to compare and eliminate programs that are duplicative, obsolete, inactive or ineffective according to their own missions and priorities. Review, according to most proposals, would take place according to a cycle of five years or more.

ANSWER SHEET

NO. _____ PART _____ TITLE OF POSITION _____

(AS GIVEN IN EXAMINATION ANNOUNCEMENT - INCLUDE OPTION, IF ANY)

CE OF EXAMINATION _____ DATE____ _____

(CITY OR TOWN)   (STATE)

RATING

USE THE SPECIAL PENCIL.   MAKE GLOSSY BLACK MARKS.

	A B C D E		A B C D E		A B C D E		A B C D E		A B C D E
1		26		51		76		101	
2		27		52		77		102	
3		28		53		78		103	
4		29		54		79		104	
5		30		55		80		105	
6		31		56		81		106	
7		32		57		82		107	
8		33		58		83		108	
9		34		59		84		109	
10		35		60		85		110	

Make only ONE mark for each answer.   Additional and stray marks may be counted as mistakes.   In making corrections, erase errors COMPLETELY.

	A B C D E		A B C D E		A B C D E		A B C D E		A B C D E
11		36		61		86		111	
12		37		62		87		112	
13		38		63		88		113	
14		39		64		89		114	
15		40		65		90		115	
16		41		66		91		116	
17		42		67		92		117	
18		43		68		93		118	
19		44		69		94		119	
20		45		70		95		120	
21		46		71		96		121	
22		47		72		97		122	
23		48		73		98		123	
24		49		74		99		124	
25		50		75		100		125	

ANSWER SHEET

TEST NO. _____ PART _____ TITLE OF POSITION _____

(AS GIVEN IN EXAMINATION ANNOUNCEMENT - INCLUDE OPTION, IF ANY)

PLACE OF EXAMINATION _____ DATE_____

(CITY OR TOWN)   (STATE)

RATING

WITHDRAWN

USE THE SPECIAL PENCIL.   MAKE GLOSSY BLACK MARKS.

	A B C D E		A B C D E		A B C D E		A B C D E		A B C D
1	:: :: :: :: ::	26	:: :: :: :: ::	51	:: :: :: :: ::	76	:: :: :: :: ::	101	:: :: :: ::
2	:: :: :: :: ::	27	:: :: :: :: ::	52	:: :: :: :: ::	77	:: :: :: :: ::	102	:: :: :: ::
3	:: :: :: :: ::	28	:: :: :: :: ::	53	:: :: :: :: ::	78	:: :: :: :: ::	103	:: :: :: ::
4	:: :: :: :: ::	29	:: :: :: :: ::	54	:: :: :: :: ::	79	:: :: :: :: ::	104	:: :: :: ::
5	:: :: :: :: ::	30	:: :: :: :: ::	55	:: :: :: :: ::	80	:: :: :: :: ::	105	:: :: :: ::
6	:: :: :: :: ::	31	:: :: :: :: ::	56	:: :: :: :: ::	81	:: :: :: :: ::	106	:: :: :: ::
7	:: :: :: :: ::	32	:: :: :: :: ::	57	:: :: :: :: ::	82	:: :: :: :: ::	107	:: :: :: ::
8	:: :: :: :: ::	33	:: :: :: :: ::	58	:: :: :: :: ::	83	:: :: :: :: ::	108	:: :: :: ::
9	:: :: :: :: ::	34	:: :: :: :: ::	59	:: :: :: :: ::	84	:: :: :: :: ::	109	:: :: :: ::
10	:: :: :: :: ::	35	:: :: :: :: ::	60	:: :: :: :: ::	85	:: :: :: :: ::	110	:: :: :: ::

Make only ONE mark for each answer.   Additional and stray marks may be counted as mistakes.   In making corrections, erase errors COMPLETELY.

	A B C D E		A B C D E		A B C D E		A B C D E		A B C D E
11	:: :: :: :: ::	36	:: :: :: :: ::	61	:: :: :: :: ::	86	:: :: :: :: ::	111	:: :: :: :: ::
12	:: :: :: :: ::	37	:: :: :: :: ::	62	:: :: :: :: ::	87	:: :: :: :: ::	112	:: :: :: :: ::
13	:: :: :: :: ::	38	:: :: :: :: ::	63	:: :: :: :: ::	88	:: :: :: :: ::	113	:: :: :: :: ::
14	:: :: :: :: ::	39	:: :: :: :: ::	64	:: :: :: :: ::	89	:: :: :: :: ::	114	:: :: :: :: ::
15	:: :: :: :: ::	40	:: :: :: :: ::	65	:: :: :: :: ::	90	:: :: :: :: ::	115	:: :: :: :: ::
16	:: :: :: :: ::	41	:: :: :: :: ::	66	:: :: :: :: ::	91	:: :: :: :: ::	116	:: :: :: :: ::
17	:: :: :: :: ::	42	:: :: :: :: ::	67	:: :: :: :: ::	92	:: :: :: :: ::	117	:: :: :: :: ::
18	:: :: :: :: ::	43	:: :: :: :: ::	68	:: :: :: :: ::	93	:: :: :: :: ::	118	:: :: :: :: ::
19	:: :: :: :: ::	44	:: :: :: :: ::	69	:: :: :: :: ::	94	:: :: :: :: ::	119	:: :: :: :: ::
20	:: :: :: :: ::	45	:: :: :: :: ::	70	:: :: :: :: ::	95	:: :: :: :: ::	120	:: :: :: :: ::
21	:: :: :: :: ::	46	:: :: :: :: ::	71	:: :: :: :: ::	96	:: :: :: :: ::	121	:: :: :: :: ::
22	:: :: :: :: ::	47	:: :: :: :: ::	72	:: :: :: :: ::	97	:: :: :: :: ::	122	:: :: :: :: ::
23	:: :: :: :: ::	48	:: :: :: :: ::	73	:: :: :: :: ::	98	:: :: :: :: ::	123	:: :: :: :: ::
24	:: :: :: :: ::	49	:: :: :: :: ::	74	:: :: :: :: ::	99	:: :: :: :: ::	124	:: :: :: :: ::
25	:: :: :: :: ::	50	:: :: :: :: ::	75	:: :: :: :: ::	100	:: :: :: :: ::	125	:: :: :: :: ::